SECOND TIME AROUND

OPTIMA

SECOND TIME AROUND

HOW DIVORCE AFFECTS
FUTURE RELATIONSHIPS

ELIZABETH MARTYN

An OPTIMA book

© Elizabeth Martyn, 1989

First published in 1989 by
Macdonald Optima, a division of
Macdonald & Co. (Publishers) Ltd

A member of Maxwell Pergamon Publishing Corporation plc

All rights reserved

No part of this publication may be reproduced,
stored in a retrieval system, or transmitted,
in any form or by any means without the prior
permission in writing of the publisher, nor be
otherwise circulated in any form of binding or
cover other than that in which it is published
and without a similar condition including this
condition being imposed on the subsequent
purchaser.

British Library Cataloguing in Publication Data

Martyn, Elizabeth
   Second time around/Elizabeth Martyn.
   1. Marriage & divorce
   I. Title
   306.8'1

ISBN 0-356-17235-X

Macdonald & Co. (Publishers) Ltd
66-73 Shoe Lane
London EC4P 4AB

Typeset in Century Schoolbook by Leaper & Gard, Bristol

Made and printed in Great Britain by
The Guernsey Press Co. Ltd., Guernsey, Channel Islands.

CONTENTS

INTRODUCTION 9

1. DAMAGED BY DIVORCE 15
   Why second marriages fail more often than first marriages

2. IRRETRIEVABLE BREAKDOWN 26
   The first marriage and its ending

3. BETWEEN THE ACTS 49
   Getting over the separation, adjusting to life alone, preparing for the future

4. JUMPING IN AGAIN 67
   The start of a new long-term relationship

5. SETTING THE BOUNDARIES 86
   Writing the rules for a successful partnership

6. THE POWER OF THE PAST 105
   Exorcising the ghost of a previous marriage

7. CHILDREN — LIVING REMINDERS 122
   Problems for stepfamilies and new families

8. HAPPILY EVER AFTER? 151

USEFUL ADDRESSES 171

For Tony, a source of constant encouragement, support, laughter and provocation, without whom ...

INTRODUCTION

The idea for *Second Time Around* sprang out of conversations I had with my second partner in our early days together. That was soon after we met, three years ago, both divorced and highly wary. I'd been married at 20, divorced at 30, and had lived alone for three years. He had been divorced for 10 years and had teenage children. Late into the night we lay awake, comparing our past experiences, talking about what was happening between us and why, and trying to work out ways of tackling our difficulties. Those conversations were often highly emotional and painful. Sometimes they ended in tears, anger or impasse, but always we came back to the fact that we wanted to be together, so somehow solutions had to be found.

It was disturbing to realise just how much our pasts had to answer for when it came to determining how we behaved in the here and now. I badly wanted the reassurance of knowing that other people had experienced this phenomenon. And as the past gradually took more of a back seat in my psyche I wanted also to offer encouragement to others who were finding it equally difficult to keep their second relationships out of danger. So I decided to write a book about it all.

My starting point was the damage caused by divorce, both practical and emotional. Obviously there is pain and sorrow whenever a relationship ends, regardless of whether the couple were married or not. Yet there are very significant differences for people who have been married. For one thing, they are more likely to have children than unmarried couples, and the existence of children often causes problems in subsequent relationships. More subtle, but equally important, are the resounding effects of bringing to an end a relationship which began with a proud and optimistic public statement. A wedding day really is

INTRODUCTION

remembered for ever: the fuss and preparation, the special dress, the church or registry office, sunshine or rain, hubbub at the reception, showers of confetti, speeches good and bad, champagne, laughter, kisses and congratulations. The whole ritual is recorded in photographs, and everyone who was there has memories of the celebrations with which that marriage began.

And there are other tangible reminders, small but still meaningful. Almost all women, and a fair number of men, will have worn a ring, blessed and given during the wedding ceremony, as an indication of their married state. And a woman will probably have changed her name. In many areas of society marriage still confers status and acceptability.

An unmarried couple has none of this. Life together often begins unannounced to the world, and it may be months before family and friends grasp the situation. Their commitment to each other is not formalised, made public, or celebrated in the same way as a wedding. And for many people marriage does signify a deeper commitment. People go into marriage hoping and expecting it to be for ever. Unmarried couples, whether they admit it or not, may well consider the bond less permanent. After all, it's not unusual to meet someone in their thirties who has lived with two, three or more people in the past, each relationship lasting for a year or two; yet it is very unusual to meet someone of that age who has been married two or three times.

Just as the beginning is different, an unmarried couple's relationship doesn't end in the same way as a marriage, even if it breaks down for similar reasons. For them the ending, though painful, can be private and quick. A married couple have the whole business of divorce to go through. Arguments over maintenance and access to children can end in a court battle. Even the most straightforward, uncontested divorce involves divulging details of the breakdown, swearing affidavits, the whole legal rigmarole. When you're divorced, you swap your wedding certificate for a decree absolute; you put away

INTRODUCTION

your wedding ring, change your name again, join the statistics. When you're divorced, people make assumptions about you, proffer judgements, disapprove, are disappointed. It's an ignominious end to a relationship that began with such high hopes, and is enough to put anyone off love and marriage for life.

That's where divorced people are when they have to set about rebuilding their lives, and that's why the first three chapters of this book are devoted to describing what happens in first marriages and immediately after. Unless you realise what people have been through before they attempt to start something new, it's impossible to understand why they have such difficulties in their subsequent relationships. Divorced people are damaged, wary, battered by their experiences. They are afraid of making another mistake, yet they want a second chance and they want to get it right.

Second relationships are tricky by definition, starting as they do in the shadow of a past failure. Yet when a second relationship works, it can be extremely rewarding, well worth the angst that goes into its forging. It can help to ease the pain of the first ending, provide stability and an opportunity for growth and greater emotional maturity. There may well be unexpected bonuses too, unlooked for in the beginning, which give the partnership greater dimensions. Perhaps a relationship with a step-child gets easier, or your partner helps you understand your own family better. Maybe you can share new interests with each other, and open up each other's horizons.

Developing a relationship takes time and some problems have no easy solution, no matter how much you talk. Making a life together second time around is a continuous process, with no foolproof recipe for guaranteed success. And everyone has times when it all seems too much effort, when your partner is just too infuriating, or you can't be bothered to argue.

In the end, each couple has to work out a unique way of co-existing: the areas of give; the dangerous places which can't take too much stress. That done, the only way

INTRODUCTION

forward is to stop theorising and analysing and get in there and live it. Set out to give each other your best and bring out the best in each other. You'll need persistence, patience and luck. All the advice in the world can't make it work for you, because only the two of you can do that for yourselves. It will be tough sometimes, but you'll know why it's worth it when you savour the easy companionship, the laughter, the love, the trust and respect on which the best relationships are based.

In researching this book, 28 people gave me lengthy interviews or completed detailed questionnaires, and I had shorter conversations with many more. The only proviso for inclusion was that people had been married in the past and were currently in a relationship — not necessarily a marriage — which they considered to be long-term. There was a wide variety of age, occupation and experience. Some had been in their second relationship for many years, others were in the early stages of adjusting to a new partner. Some had been divorced a second time and were now in a third relationship, or living alone again. Many had children. Sometimes one partner only in a couple was prepared to talk; women were more willing to talk than men. Some were my friends, or friends of friends; others responded to press advertisements or came to me via the National Stepfamily Association or Relate.

I would like to thank them all for sharing their experiences so frankly. It was a privilege to be allowed such an insight into your struggles and a share in your joys and disappointments, and I wish you success and happiness in your relationships in the future. I would also like to thank the friends, colleagues and acquaintances who were generous with the words of encouragement and enthusiasm that are such music to a lone writer's ears!

And finally, to people embarking nervously on a second relationship, or newly divorced and filled with trepidation at the idea of new involvement: read what others who have tried it have to say and take heart.

Throughout the following chapters, many people describe the problems they have had, and how they have gone about dealing with them. Much of what they say makes good sense, although it's not always comfortable reading. Their conclusions and advice in Chapter 8 are based on the reality of the hard struggle to make new relationships work. There's no magic formula, no list of numbered points to follow, no possible way that success can be guaranteed. Every couple is different, and there are as many potential pitfalls as there are people. Expect it to be tough and you won't be disappointed. Expect it to be hugely rewarding as well and with courage, perseverance and a large measure of luck, you'll not be disappointed there, either.

If you have found the right person, and worked out your needs together, it is possible to make the relationship the success you want it to be, and to use the experience from your first marriage and divorce in a positive way to make that happen. Good luck!

1.
DAMAGED BY DIVORCE

Why second marriages fail more often than first marriages

Few people emerge from a divorce unscarred. After such an emotionally devastating experience you'd think most of them would be decidedly wary of setting off down the same path again. Far from it. Although many spend months or years living without a partner, waiting for the wounds to heal or a suitable candidate to show up, eventually the need for stability, companionship and comfort of a close relationship has to be met. Even the most jaded divorcees, those who said firmly 'never again', suddenly find the energy and enthusiasm to embark on the search for a brand new partner. Undaunted by the trauma of a broken marriage, about half of divorcees remarry within five years of their divorce, and many others cohabit. Sooner or later, the majority of divorced people (particularly men), find themselves another permanent partner.

More divorced people enter the marriage market all the time. In 1986, the population included nearly two million divorcees, although the same year did see a 7,000 drop in the 1985 record of 175,000 divorces. The rate of remarriage increases in proportion to that of divorce, so, for a couple marrying today there's a one-in-three chance that one partner has taken the vows before, while at one in every six weddings it's the second attempt for both.

WHAT CHANCE OF SUCCESS?

The outlook after divorce certainly isn't one of a long and solitary future. People are astonishingly resilient and many throw themselves back into the fray of man–woman encounters fairly soon after separating. It says a lot for human optimism that so many are prepared to take the risk and commit themselves to another relationship regardless of what has gone before. But although the lessons learned ought to give divorced people a head start in the successful marriage stakes, sad to say, the reverse is true. Almost a quarter of divorces involve one party who has been divorced before. And the marriage of a pair of divorcees has a higher chance of ending on the rocks than that of two first-timers. Perhaps the rush back to togetherness is sometimes prompted more by an urgent need for the 'safety' of coupledom than the advent of a suitably compatible relationship.

WHAT GOES WRONG?

First-hand experience of how a relationship can break down catastrophically doesn't always seem to help divorced people see straight when they're lining up to take the plunge again. Why is it so hard for second relationships to flourish? There are no proven answers, no research-backed statistics about why there is this high rate of breakdown. Everyone's experience is different, but while there are no rules, there are some factors that emerge strongly and repeatedly.

Fear of living alone
It's understandable that people who have been used to a married existence miss it very much and find life in the single world difficult and lonely. The danger comes when a desperate and lonely divorcee seizes on the first possible partner who happens along, blithely ignoring any danger signals.

Helen, a social worker, moved in with Bill immediately

after her 36-year-old husband left her for a 17-year-old girl.

> We met on a course, and I moved in with him within three months. Bill's chief attraction was that he was in the same boat — his wife had fallen for someone else and he had lost home and three children. I fell for him like a ton of bricks — tall, handsome and very sad! Irresistible to me. Later, when legally free to marry — and pretty disillusioned — I considered *not* marrying, but was too cowardly to live alone. I couldn't imagine myself on my own, a separate individual. I wasn't thinking clearly, I felt trapped and panic-stricken. We are still together 15 years later, but there have been endless problems.

For Diana, the consequences of marrying 'on the rebound' have been disastrous. She met her second husband six months after her first husband had left her for another woman.

> I hated being single and felt very insecure. I can't handle freedom, and didn't like any of it. I didn't go out until I was persuaded to go to Gingerbread and I met my second husband there the first time I went. I moved in with him six months later and we lived together for 18 months before we married. Problems arose with his two children immediately. One left home, the other will not speak to me. Money has been a problem as he doesn't seem keen to assume financial responsibility. He is extremely lazy around the house, quiet and hard-hearted, uncommunicative. I feel I have made a total mess of relationships. This one has been another mistake, and I think we will be divorced.

Even people who wanted to separate can suffer unexpectedly when they find themselves no longer part of a couple. Malcolm, who left his wife with great relief in his mid-thirties, found 'The evenings were often lonely. I missed sharing the events of the day with someone. In a funny way I even missed the rows!' Eventually he moved in with a girlfriend, 'partly for companionship. I wasn't in love with her, and never considered it a permanent arrangement.' After 18 months he returned to living alone, and found it 'a preferable way of life to living with the wrong person, despite the occasional loneliness.'

Children
It stands to reason that as so many divorces involve children, very many new relationships must have to accommodate them, sometimes to the extent of providing them with a home. It's a far-reaching factor that easily gets overlooked early on, but which never goes away. Perhaps more than anything else, dealing with someone else's children requires maturity, acceptance and understanding — a pretty tall order. The frequency with which problems over children are mentioned as contributing if not at least to serious problems, to the breakdown of a second relationship, reflect this.

The legacy of the past
All partnerships are beset by difficulties at times, and whenever two individuals get together a new set of frictions, incompatibilities and potential problems is unleashed. There are practical problems concerning the simple mechanics of readjusting to a dual life. And there is an extra hurdle: each failed marriage produces a burden of emotional history which is brought into subsequent relationships, can affect them profoundly, and yet often goes unrecognised. In the pleasure of a new romance, the pain of previous separation may seem to be forgotten. But is it so easily shrugged off? On the surface, everything seems different with a new partner, but deep in the subconscious, old feelings are stirring. Few marriages end calmly. Grief, distress, regret, anger, bitterness, fury, frustration — any or all of these powerful feelings have to be worked through in the healing process, which can take years and may never really be completed. Until those

feelings have been allowed to run their course, the first marriage is still alive and able to threaten a new liaison.

During a phase of living alone after a divorce, it may well be possible to suppress or deny past pain, or to think that it has been confronted and dealt with. But the start of a new relationship offers regular opportunities for reminders of forgotten anguish. After all, in terms of domestic co-existence, one relationship is much like another. Days and weeks follow roughly the same pattern, meals are eaten, people go to work and return, stay in for the evening or go out, take holidays, do the chores, just as in any household. Each situation is a potential trigger for old patterns of behaviour to reestablish themselves. They may be forgotten for weeks on end, but now and then they surface. And if both partners are divorced, then they have the phantoms of two past marriages to contend with.

How does this legacy of former feeling manifest itself? It can happen in many ways, subtle or obvious. The divorced are no longer 'virgins'. They are full of responses learned in their first marriage, and, although they may think they have changed, the chances are you need only scratch the surface and out it all comes. The woman whose first husband was unfaithful has lost the ability to trust; the man whose wife belittled him strikes out defensively at the smallest hint of criticism. These people bear deep scars and their old hurts can emerge as inexplicable responses to their partner's actions, as past resentments, fears and vulnerabilities come surging back. If this goes unrecognised and unacknowledged, it can seriously undermine a new relationship, which, once weakened, may eventually collapse.

Lowered tolerance

Second marriages that are going to fail tend to do so more quickly than first marriages, which indicates that re-marriers are less tolerant, less willing to put up with unacceptable behaviour, quicker to throw in the towel when things aren't going well. Why should this be? One answer is that people are very reluctant to endure a long, drawn-out disintegration, and would rather get out fast than hang around and wait for things to go from bad to worse. Charlotte stayed in her first marriage for five years, even though serious problems were evident from the outset. She says of her second marriage:

> Before my divorce, I'd bend over backwards to keep things calm. If we did have a big bust up I'd do anything to get us back on an even keel, which I wouldn't do now. That doesn't mean I love Nick less than my first husband, because I love him more. It is a more mature relationship, but I won't tolerate any nonsense again. If there was the least inkling of anything like last time — violence, or infidelity — I'd be off like a shot.'

Another reason for the speedier breakdown of second marriages might be that people are less afraid of the alternative. David, who stayed with his first wife for ten years, agrees:

> I know what it's like to be stuck in a dead relationship for years, because you're afraid to leave. And I know too what life is like on my own. I know I can cope perfectly well, it's not something to be scared of. If things went wrong this time, I wouldn't stick it out for so long. Of course I'd make an effort to save the relationship, but I wouldn't sacrifice another five or six years of my life.

LONG-TERM EFFECTS OF DIVORCE: BAD AND GOOD

'You'll never get over it'; 'you'll soon bounce back'; 'it takes two years to recover'; 'plenty more fish in the sea'. There can't be many divorced people who haven't had all these well-meaning platitudes heaped on them by concerned friends and relatives. Generally, though, you won't find people who've been through a divorce subscribing to the notion that it's similar to a bout of flu; something you get over, leave behind, rapidly forget.

Harriet, 40, a writer, has been separated for two years and says, 'Though mostly I feel OK, I suffer a lot from nostalgia and a sense of attachment to my husband, no matter who else is on the scene.' And Rachel, a 36-year-old mother of twins, who had an acrimonious separation from her first husband eight years ago says:

> There are lots of difficult emotions and grieving to deal with after a divorce, and if you don't do that you'll be unable to make the next relationship successfully. You can put fullstops in your life by getting a piece of paper which says you're divorced and allows you to go on to the next stage, but don't think you've shut the door and shouldn't or couldn't go back, because you will. Hardly a day goes by when I don't think about my first husband, or some aspect of our life together, even if only fleetingly. I think it's right to acknowledge that the past is a very important part of the present.

It's easy to underestimate the damaging effects of divorce. For many, the experience is one of the most devastating and distressing that they have ever endured, even if they deny having suffered. Feelings of guilt, inadequacy, failure, social stigma and shame are all common, even among people who wanted to escape from a bad marriage. Although relief is the emotion most frequently expressed at the end of the line, it is often understandably tempered with sadder, less positive feelings: since most marriages start out with the greatest of expectations, it is sad when those high hopes come crashing down. And it certainly seems unlikely that anyone who has shared his or her life so closely with another can fail to be marked emotionally when the relationship is finally sundered.

However, the experience and fact of a divorce can also have positive and good effects. Wendy, now separated for the second time, says:

> I learnt a lot about life from my first marriage — I find it hard to be regretful. I don't wish that things had

worked out and that we'd stayed together, because I've learned so much more about life from my second partner.

Tom, 49, was divorced 10 years before he met his present partner. He feels he has gained valuable insights into the lives of others as a result of his divorce: 'I understand other people's relationships, their griefs (marital or bereavement), their concern and love for their children.' For Sue, 25, the insight has been into herself.

I didn't begin to grow up until I left my husband six years ago. I don't believe it would have been possible to develop within that marriage as I have done since. My personality and creativity were being gradually stifled out of existence.

Russell, a company director aged 41, makes frequent, happy comparisons between present and past: 'I appreciate my current life with my girlfriend more as a result of my first marriage, as I know what the alternative could have been.'

There are few fates worse than being trapped in a terrible marriage. Better by far to escape, battle-scarred but free, than to stay put and resign yourself to a life of misery until death intervenes. If you're exceptionally lucky you might even achieve a better relationship with your ex-partner once you no longer have to battle it out day by day. Harriet: 'I feel friendship for my husband, and affection. We get on better now we are separated.' Madeleine, 38, a lecturer, whose marriage lasted 15 troubled years finds, 'A relaxed, friendly atmosphere in our occasional business dealings.'

For many, the liberation of divorce gives them a long-awaited opportunity to discover themselves, fulfil their own wants and needs and live their own life. Laura, who left a violent husband when she was 35 says, 'I enjoyed immensely the opportunity to read again and listen to music whenever I wanted, without being distracted to give attention for the sake of it.' Rachel was so relieved that the misery of her marriage was over that

> Living alone was wonderful, and I loved it. There must have been times when I was lonely, but I'd been so lonely in my marriage. I never felt anything like that devastating loneliness when I lived alone, and I was very relieved not to have Sam in tow because he was like some terrible ball and chain.

Tom relished 'the freedom to explore life outside the home, notably art galleries and antique shops.' Divorce can undoubtedly provide great potential for personal growth and happiness for individuals, as well as leaving the way free for them to form new and better relationships in the future. But in order to do that, some lessons have to be absorbed.

LEARNING AND CHANGING

Why is it so hard to learn from experience? What demon flies in the face of our better judgement, and drives us headlong into the same snakepits over and over again? Twice-divorced Kate, now 46, says 'Both times I married I thought as I signed the little book that I was doing something ridiculous. But nothing on earth would have stopped me.'

This self-destructive element of human nature, the close-your-eyes-jump-and-damn-the-consequences syndrome is commonplace, even among people who usually exercise careful judgement in other areas of their lives. No matter how many people share their experiences and give pointers along the road to success, there are always those subconscious factors to contend with: the search for security or a parental figure; despair of ever finding a partner; boredom; the baby time-bomb. All these can be very powerful in over-riding common sense and propelling people into ill-considered relationships. In the end, no one can tell anyone else how to make a decision, or what to choose. Individuals have to weigh it up for themselves and if they decide to ignore the warning signs and carry on regardless — well, who's to say what the outcome will be? People survive in the most unlikely liaisons, after all.

For all that, it is interesting that people in unhappy second relationships often claim to have learned nothing from the first experiences, while those who are happier often point to the importance of learning from experience. Diana, who is gearing up for her second divorce: 'What lessons did I learn from my first marriage? None unfortunately. I have the tendency to make the same mistakes again.' And Hilary, on her own again after two failed marriages says 'The cliche that we learn by our mistakes is not true. I seem to marry men because I want to change their lives and make them happy. I hope I've broken the habit!' And Jenny, who is unhappy in her second marriage:

> I was scared of going it alone and security did play a large part. I think I married again because of fear, fear of being unable to cope alone. Security appeared more satisfying than standing on my own two feet. People always seem to have dominated my life and this is still true of my second husband. I feel very angry with myself for my own weakness.

Among those who rated their second relationships a success, many had learned the value of tolerance and acceptance from their first experiences, although some thought that this was something which would have come with age anyway. Madeleine says:

> I've changed by becoming more tolerant of, and sympathetic to, other people's problems. I was never a very 'judgemental' person anyway, but encountering the odd bigot has reminded me how little people can know of the true nature of others' lives, and how even less should they make judgements.

Alan, whose first marriage lasted 11 years, says, 'I hope I'm more tender, less selfish, more patient ... but a lot of that comes with more years too!' Veronica, who was dominated by an 'utterly insensitive' husband for 19 years before escaping, says, 'I am more confident, but that might have come with age anyway.'

The consensus among these people is that it does seem to be possible to change, and for repeating patterns to be broken, but it's not easy. Harriet says:

> I don't think I've changed enough probably, though I would now be very unwilling to jeopardise this relationship by the kind of behaviour I indulged in during my marriage: i.e. affairs. I can't see any reason to want them anyway. The need was a product of that relationship and this one is different. I don't believe in patterns necessarily repeating themselves.

David, 38, has found it extraordinarily hard:

> I know why I react in certain ways, when something Barbara does reminds me of my first wife. Just knowing it isn't enough; it's learning to respond to Barbara as herself, without the past getting in the way, that's so difficult. I keep trying, and gradually as the past fades it does get easier.

2.
IRRETRIEVABLE BREAKDOWN
The first marriage and its ending

In order to get something positive from the experience of divorce, it's vital, though painful, to examine the first marriage and learn from its mistakes: how it began; what went wrong; the experiences that coloured hopes, dictated responses and behaviour, and turned the two partners into the people they have become by the time they embark on successive relationships.

WHY MARRY?

The choice of a marriage partner is one of the most far-reaching decisions made in a lifetime, yet for many young people parental pressure and desire for independence are more compelling motivations than any personal attractions of their intended mate. 'Love' or 'being in love' is an influence for only a minority. It's surprising, considering the popularity of romantic films and fiction, to realise that the thought uppermost in many a young newlywed's head is, 'Thank God I don't have to go back home to mother', rather than 'I can't wait to share my life with this wonderful person.'

Expectations of married life are often wildly unrealistic first time around, with people looking to their partners to fulfil their every need, emotional and practical. There's often an astonishing disregard for basic compatability on an intellectual, sexual or emotional level, and a failure to consider what both parties want from the marriage and whether their hopes coincide.

Many young people don't have a clue what to expect from marriage, and find out the hard way how much — or little — is on offer. Colin married at 21, safe in the belief that: 'marriage was an end in itself. We were in love, we got married, therefore we would live happily ever after.'

Others come up with a list of requirements that could only be met by a super-spouse, and are then horribly disappointed when their partner turns out to be human. Maggie, now 58: 'I was looking for everything in a husband! Lover, life companion, friend, a source of fulfilment and growth.' Diana: 'I was looking for someone who could look after me and love me. My views of marriage were totally idealistic.' Alan: 'I wanted companionship, sex, ultimately children, a lifelong partnership with a partner who had looks, intelligence and tenderness — not necessarily in that order, but a reasonable mix.' Harriet:

> I expected companionship, friendship, security, a family, a replacement for my parents who were both dead, a bit of fun. I wanted my partner to be friend, lover, companion and also subconsciously a lot more: brother, mother, father, complete support system.

Some shopping list! Yet there don't seem to be any hard and fast rules as to why some couples get enough of what they want to make the relationship work and others don't. Doubtless numerous people marry in similar circumstances to those described in this chapter and *don't* end up in the divorce courts. Luck, adaptability and general disposition have a great deal to do with it, and one couple's recipe for disaster will keep another pair battling on together for 50 years. The question for those who don't stay the course is not so much who did wrong by whom, but rather what effect their experience had on them, and whether they can use it to avoid falling into the same traps next time.

IRRETRIEVABLE BREAKDOWN

PARENTAL PRESSURES

Our first impressions of marriage come from observing our parents' relationship. What we see inevitably affects our own expectations. Like it or not, parents have a powerful influence on our choice of partner. Whether we marry to escape from them, to please them, or to demonstrate our rebelliousness by choosing an unacceptable mate, we are still succumbing to the power of family opinion — and if things go wrong quite probably storing up a good dose of trouble and resentment for the future.

Part of the reason why parents exert such strong control over first marriages is that often the couple are barely out of their teens, and one or both may still be living at home. To take an extreme example, Kate met her first husband, Jack, when she was 13. He was 10 years older, and her mother did not approve.

> I met Jack on a putting green. He whistled and I responded. I was besotted, as one is at 13, and the following year I went back desperately to hunt him down. We went out together in secret for quite a long while. But then we had to stop seeing each other because my mother got wind of the relationship. She gave me a thorough cross-examination and I came out with the whole story. She did not approve of the goings-on at all; she was prepared to sue him because I was under age. It was all very unpleasant, and my relationship with my mother was ruined as a result.
>
> I went on seeing Jack surreptitiously and played truant from school. Then I stupidly told a neighbour I was about to elope with him, she told my mother and there was a family conference, from which my father was excluded. I think mum realised then that there wasn't much she could do about it. She made Jack and I swear on the Bible to be totally platonic for the next year while he saved up some money and then we would get married. And that was what happened.

During the Fifties, Sixties and even early Seventies, when

many of these first marriages were taking place, it was far less acceptable than it is today for a couple to live together unwed. The thought didn't cross Kate's mind: 'Marriage was the right and proper thing to do in 1959. One didn't live with a man unless one wanted to be tarred and feathered for ever, figuratively speaking. And I couldn't go on living at home any longer, because it had become intolerable.' Madeleine, 22 when she married in 1972, felt the same, 'I married in order to create a secure and happy environment, my own home having been strife-torn. Also, it would have greatly upset my parents if I had simply lived with him.' And, similarly, for Alan: 'I was 24 and she was 22. We would have said at the time that we wanted to marry because we loved one another (in 1962 living together out of wedlock was not yet so acceptable as it is today). With hindsight, I wanted to assert independence from my background.'

The search for freedom from parental restrictions often overrides all other considerations. Rhoda, who married at 20:

> I didn't get on with my parents and marriage was the ideal opportunity to get away from home. And his parents were beginning to wonder when we would get married. I knew right at the beginning the marriage wouldn't work. I stuck it out for two years, but I did have quite a few affairs in the meantime.

Veronica, who stayed unhappily married for 19 years, expressed her doubts to her mother before the wedding:

> I wasn't mature enough to know what to expect from marriage, or to fathom out what I wanted in a partner. I knew there were problems prior to the marriage, in fact three weeks before the wedding day I wanted to call it off, but was persuaded to go ahead by my mother.

Parents often use cultural and religious levers to encourage their children to conform. Laura married at 23 because, 'I thought I might have been in love, and needed desperately to leave home. Also, from my mother, "He's a nice, clean living, decent Jewish boy, and who else would have you?"' And Rachel, another good Jewish girl who got married at 25 to a man 13 years older than herself:

> My parents had an engagement party for us. They were pleased because they liked him. He was very charming. I think my father might have had reservations, he has very good antennae, but if he did he was probably stifled. They were extremely pleased that I was getting involved with somebody of the right religion for once. At least I wouldn't have to fight that battle, and I think that was a reason why I suspended my usually critical judgement.

Tom, too, was a victim of a religion-based upbringing and education when he married at 28: 'I decided to marry because it was time to settle down. She was Catholic, as I was, and available. I wanted a settled home with children and I was looking for someone to provide this home.'

Getting married to please mother is one side of the coin; the other is to set out deliberately to shock and antagonise her. Wendy's first marriage only lasted five months:

> From the age of about 15 I thought I must get engaged and married. He was my first boyfriend when I left school, and we were like kids. I wanted to make his mother jealous. It was just the thrill of surprising and upsetting her. I'd only been married a few weeks when I thought, 'Oh dear, I don't want to stay here.' I was bored, I didn't enjoy going to bed with him. I was very, very immature. After about four months I met Gerard, the chap I married many years later. We were both very attracted, flirted madly and then eloped. Gerard forced me to do it. He said, 'Go home now and pack.' I said, 'I can't just leave him,' and he said 'Yes you can, leave him a note and I'll wait in the pub for you.' I hardly remember how my husband reacted. He changed the locks, and my mother and aunt were angry because of the wedding presents. That was all I knew.

SEX AND PREGNANCY

The same era that dictated 'marriage or nothing' was also harsh in its condemnation of premarital sex. Marianne, who was divorced in 1985, explains the theory:

> I would suggest that one of the major causes for the current divorce rate is the 'conditioning' many people received when growing up in the Fifties and Sixties. At that time girls were told that to sleep with a man who was not your husband was 'just not done' — downright wicked in fact. Marriage was the aim for all girls, as not only did they want to be acceptable, but also to find out what 'doing it' was about! I would not encourage sleeping around, but I strongly believe that sexual expression should only be part of the reason for getting married. To make love to someone you truly care for is wonderful, but a partnership requires far more than that.

The result of sexual ignorance and inexperience was that many marriages brought to bed unpractised and physically incompatible partners. Both Wendy's first and second husbands were sexually inadequate: 'The third man I lived with was the opposite of any sort of man I'd ever liked before. I'd always gone out with men who were larger than life, domineering, all dreadful in bed. I didn't have a good sex life until I was 34!'

Madeleine's first marriage was blighted by sexual difficulties: 'My husband married me because it was a way of disguising a sexual identity problem. Sexual failure was one of the main problems, because he had a failed and unadmitted previous homosexual relationship.' Sue's problem was slightly different.

> Before we were married our sex life was great. I was 18 and a virgin when we met, but took to sex like a duck to water! It always had to be clandestine and hurried though, and we were rarely able to spend a whole night together. That was one area of our relationship I thought

could only improve after we were married. I was looking forward to being able to make love more often, whenever we felt like it. So I was appalled when Daniel cooled off towards me, instantly. Right from the first months of marriage we were having sex no more than twice a week, always in bed under the covers, after 11pm, generally with the lights off. It was as if he lost interest in sex as soon as it was permitted. I felt dreadfully hurt and rejected, my self-esteem took a real bashing. Over the nine years we were together the situation gradually worsened, until eventually he wouldn't undress in front of me, told me to cover myself up if I wandered around naked, locked the door when he had a bath, and only wanted sex once a month or so. I think a lot of our other problems stemmed from that, because even when things were fairly good, I always felt frustrated and rejected; not wanted as a woman.

Before the days when reliable contraception was readily available to unmarried people, many couples paid for their experiments with sex by finding themselves precipitated down the aisle by an unwanted pregnancy. Jenny, an occupational therapist, was 18 when she got married.

We married because I was pregnant, and I wanted security for the child. I realised on the very first day that there were problems. The main one was my resentment at having to get married. It was difficult to discuss things because we were so immature. All I did was lose my temper and shout my resentment. He was very placid. I behaved violently towards him, and tried to live a single life, having boyfriends outside the marriage. My husband knew about them, and I had little interest in sex with him. Eventually he found someone else and asked me to leave.

Pregnancy plus infatuation swept Judith into an ill-advised marriage.

I was 24 and he was 33 when we married. He'd been married before for 12 years, and had three children. His wife just walked out one day and left him with the children. He kept trying to find her, and they didn't divorce until he wanted to marry me because I was pregnant. I thought that motherhood, love and marriage were the answers to everything and that once we were married everything in the garden would be rosy! I really was on cloud nine. I desperately wanted to care for him and all his children. But after two and a half years the problems started. He felt he had to go to bed with every woman who came along and he had great fun screwing all my girlfriends and telling me about it. There were eight altogether. Gradually, over about six years, the infatuation wore off and I chucked him out with his latest conquest.

Judith may have been lucky to make such a swift escape. Often marriages that begin with an unwanted pregnancy drag on for far longer, shakily glued together by the children that caused them to happen. Harry stayed put for 16 years before he reached breaking point.

We should never have got married, it was a shotgun wedding of the Sixties, which was a dreadful mistake. But it went on, and eventually we had three children . . . From very early on I realised my marriage was not correct. I was too young at 19. Over the next four or five years I changed, I became myself and not what I was at 18 or 19. Before I was about 25 I was still learning who and what I was. We weren't ideally matched and didn't really have that much in common, the only bond was the children. We grew apart and our outlooks and feelings were different. After a few years I started having mistresses. I never quite got round to leaving because I never had enough reason. The alternative didn't appeal that much, and there were always the children. But in end I got fed up with living an open lie.

It was by no means unknown for women to use 'pregnancy' to encourage a reluctant swain to do the decent thing. Philip, now in his late fifties, had only known his wife for six weeks when:

> She said she was pregnant, and in those days there was nothing for it but to get married. She then had a 'miscarriage' on the honeymoon. I think now that she believed my family had plenty of money and the right connections. Before we were married she claimed to be a German baroness. That should have put me on my guard, but my mother and sister encouraged the match. I subsequently discovered that she was the illegitimate daughter of an obscure German count!

HOW IMPORTANT IS LOVE?

In the stories quoted there's been precious little mention of love — that supposedly fundamental ingredient of a happy marriage. But what of the minority who *do* confess to finding themselves in love's grip? Unfortunately, it's debatable whether being 'in love' in the traditional, hearts and flowers, mode helps anyone to make a sensible decision when they are considering marriage. And sometimes love, although genuinely and perhaps passionately felt, is not strong enough to withstand the compromises and disillusionments common in the early years of a marriage.

Kate went into her first marriage full of romantic ideals.

> I was 17 when I married him. It was lovely because I got my freedom. I cooked all the dishes that mother wouldn't let me cook at home, got in my weird furniture and my cat, and people came and saw us and sat up all night talking. I had a normal teenage life with Jack, which was very nice. I was passionately in love with him . . .

But the dream was shattered when she discovered he had concealed serious debts:

> I found out soon enough how deeply he was in debt when the letters started to arrive. The first I duly handed to him, it not being my policy to interfere with my husband's mail, and he went away looking terribly worried. So I changed my policy rapidly, intercepted the next one and found out that we were about £400 in debt, which was a lot of money then. I confronted him, and said: 'I've made a commitment and I'm prepared to stick by it; is there anything else you want to tell me, because if so tell me now.' And he said 'No, no, it's all right, that's it.' But about a week later another letter arrived about another couple of hundred . . . We were together five years in all, but it wasn't the same after that. The freedom was nice, the social life was great, I was working and had an exciting, stimulating job. But I was on my own then within the marriage, I felt.

For Harriet, love failed to sustain a marriage against the sexual difficulties that beset it.

> We married for love, because it meant we were serious. It seemed very much the right thing to do. The problems began after the birth of my daughter, two years into the marriage. A painful, difficult birth led to sexual problems, pain on intercourse and a gradual withdrawal from sex which had never been great anyway . . . My husband was unwilling to discuss the problem of premature ejaculation. His attitude was that all men conducted sexual intercourse in this way and it was my problem, not his. Affairs ensued. So did resentment, and lack of sexual communication led to other problems.

For Maggie, the problems were more immediate, despite her high hopes and optimism.

> We were in love and had shared idealism. We took great pleasure in each other's company. There was a sense of the world opening up because of him. I found him very intelligent and stimulating. But I realised immediately

that there were problems, in fact some were apparent before we married. The main trouble was his sexual jealousy, which extended to the period before we had met. He had little reason for it — I was completely faithful all our marriage. It was an unresolved oedipal obsession, which eventually led him to shun me sexually and to dislike me. My problem was of finding it difficult to live an independent life within the confines of marriage.

Charlotte, too, had misgivings before her marriage, suspecting that her husband-to-be tended towards violence, but allowed herself to be swept away by romance and excitement.

> I was very much in love with Steve at the time. I was frightened of losing him, I wanted a home and family. I wanted romance too. He was romantic, and I liked him because he was different and exciting.
>
> I didn't realise for a long time that I disliked Steve as a person. I was very attracted to him, and didn't recognise the problems as such at the time. He'd been engaged before and his fiancée got fed up with the drinking and violence and broke it off. I knew that had happened — he and his family joked about it, things like 'Sandra says you broke her arm' — but it was a joke, and I thought, oh she must have been some neurotic woman. Even when he hit me outside a party, I persuaded myself that it was my fault, that I drove him to it because I was such a pain. I'd never come across violence before, and I always felt it must be because of me. He used to say 'I've talked to people and they say they'd have done much worse to you if you'd said what you said to me.' I always tried to understand why he'd hit me, which was ridiculous. But he was the first person I'd fallen in love with who'd fallen in love with me, and even though I was only 20 I'd begun to think it would never happen.
>
> People seem to be able to sustain love for many years in

the most unhappy relationships. Wendy fell madly for Gerard, who would plague her life for years to come, but with whom she remained in love through thick and thin for many years.

> I moved in with him straight away. I was delighted with him. But it was always a difficult relationship, I was crying and sobbing from the first week because he was so cruel. He'd take all my money and lock me up and go out and spend it all on booze. Or if he was being nice he'd ring me and say I want you to cook me something special tonight, so I'd do all the shopping, cook the bloody thing and then he wouldn't come home, sometimes not for days, because he was out drinking. But because I was used to being dominated by my mother I felt quite comfortable in this unpleasant relationship with Gerard and put up with it for years, always wanting him to love me.
> From the age of 21 to 30 my life with him changed every few weeks or months. He was in America for a year, when I went out with lots of other people and so did he. But we'd always ring each other and say we loved each other. Then eventually, after nine years, he was offered the tenancy of a pub — if he had a wife. So we got married. I wanted him to want me. At last he was going to marry me, that was a major statement. We had an amazing party that lasted a couple of days.
> I married him without misgivings and then I had a baby. There were real problems during the pregnancy, when he had one or two sexual, drunken orgies on our premises, when I was feeling very vulnerable. Afterwards, when I was suffering from hormonal depression after the birth he was very unkind. I asked him for help and he said 'you'd think no one had ever had a baby before', and just left me to it. I used to drive to Beachy Head every day and stand there with my baby in my arms and think, I wish I could jump. I vowed then to leave him. I certainly did love him, but I stopped quite soon after marrying him and becoming pregnant.

EARLY WARNINGS

Terminal problems are usually evident to one partner, at least, within the first five years of marriage. What's amazing is how often people are well aware of the potential danger areas much sooner than that, often before the marriage, and frequently within weeks or even days of the ceremony. Entering into marriage full of secret misgivings is described over and over again. Rhoda: 'It was a disaster from the word go. We tried to make it work, but I was too young, although I didn't realise that at the time, and he was too introverted. I needed someone to bring me out and he didn't do that for me. So after a while I strayed away.'

Charlotte didn't have to wait long for her worst fears to be realised.

> A few weeks after we were married I started to find empty brandy bottles. I knew he was a heavy drinker but I didn't know he was drinking that much. And I took the attitude that I wouldn't blame him because I didn't want to be the kind of wife who gave him a hard time. So I tried to understand. But then the violence started to get worse and worse. It was always connected with the drinking, although I think he is a violent person anyway. He would pick a row. It didn't happen a lot, but when it did it was quite bad. I had to take a week off work once, because my face was bruised. But I was so frightened he would leave. I still loved him very much, in a possessive way . . .
>
> I found out quite a while later that he had had other women right through our marriage. I was so naive — I thought he was so much in love with me. I even found a pair of knickers in his suitcase once and he said someone had put them there as a joke. He said 'Do you think if I was having an affair I'd do something so careless?' And that seemed to make sense.

For Russell, whose marriage lasted four years, the writing was on the wall well before the wedding: 'The relationship was already rapidly deteriorating by the time she fell pregnant, which was the reason for our marriage. The main problem was money and her desire to live beyond our means. There were also difficulties with the daughter from her first marriage.' Laura heard warning bells before wedding bells too, but closed her ears to them.

> I realised there were problems even during our engagement. There was a lack of communication and we hardly ever agreed. I tried to discuss this, but my husband didn't acknowledge that difficulties existed. I always found the words to tackle a situation, but he was unable to respond adequately and then used violence in frustration.

Joanna had only known Ian for six months and quickly regretted the rash mood that led her to make it permanent.

> We married on impulse. I hoped for security, fidelity, freedom from the dating rat-race, but the problems began almost immediately. He underwent a complete character change as soon as we were married, became violent and disappeared for days on end. I tried to talk about it, but he seemed to have become a complete madman and often hit me. In the end he started to mix with some very shady characters and was having an affair, so I threw him out, which took some doing. I felt a fool for having been taken in by him.

Diana, who admits to marrying in order to leave home, says: 'I realised on the first day of the marriage that he was not communicative. We were totally incompatible, he was too quiet and unable to relate to anyone but computer people. He was violent, and this escalated from the beginning of the marriage.' Madeleine too found her hopes disappointed very early on.

> There were problems within a few months. I'd hoped for

IRRETRIEVABLE BREAKDOWN

a husband who had a warmth of personality, with whom I could enjoy shared interests. But my husband lacked warmth and I became aware that, whereas I was always adapting to his interests and requirements, he found it more difficult to consider mine.

Tom tried twice to break off his engagement but caved in in the face of his fiancée's protests. 'The problems began in earnest after three months of marriage. We were incompatible, with different intellectual and emotional needs and levels. After a year I suggested divorce. She was upset, I relented. No further discussion.'

Rachel married and moved to Africa to live with her husband Sam. She had to cope with a foreign environment as well as problems from Sam's first marriage.

It wasn't plain sailing from quite early on, although our situation was one where it was quite hard for me to make normal judgements because I was out of my social and geographical context. I was in a strange country, in his house, and moving in a strange social circle which I disliked. He had divorced his first wife there and she had remarried a younger man. Sam and she were still fighting out the custody battle over their son who was about nine. The son visited for several weeks at a time which was very difficult because he didn't want to let Sam out of his sight and certainly didn't want me coming between them. Although I understood that, I felt that Sam wasn't prepared to take my needs seriously at all. When I look back on it I think he was quite cynically playing us off against each other, just as he had done in his first marriage. I remember feeling very isolated.

GROWING APART

Misguided choices of partner soon become apparent: a woman with a deep need for financial security shackles herself to a profligate spender; a home-loving man settles down with a restless, itchy-footed woman. Recipes for disaster? Of course — and the rot is quick to set in. But sometimes a partnership can seem fine on the surface and survive quite contentedly for some time before things start to decline. Problems such as infidelity or violence can take a while to emerge, as they did for Lynn: 'I realised there were problems in the second year of marriage. I was pregnant, not too well, and had a demanding job. And he began having affairs with other women while away from home on business.'

For many people the problem is less specific. Growing feelings of frustration, non-fulfilment or boredom all contribute to the 'growing apart' that is often given as a reason for a separation. Personalities develop and alter dramatically through the twenties, and there's no guarantee that a couple will take off in the same direction, or find themselves as compatible at 30 as they were at 19. Eleanor sums it up. Married at 20, she'd had enough after six years. 'I was bored. I grew up and changed. And then I became attracted to my present partner. He is the complete opposite to my first husband.'

THE TRAUMA OF MARRIAGE BREAKDOWN

Divorce is often talked about lightly, but for most people it is an agonising experience. Just because the problems often start early on, the marriage doesn't necessarily end quickly, and many people put up with years of misery until they finally make the break. Hilary, now 60, looks back:

> My first marriage lasted 22 years, not because it was happy but because I had no money of my own with which to escape and I had three children. My first visit to a solicitor was in 1954 when it was gently pointed out to me that unless I could produce a witness who had seen my husband strike me three times, within 48 hours, I would not be able to get a divorce on the grounds of cruelty. If I deserted him he would not be liable to support me or my children. Such was the law

pre-1968. So I endured another 17 years of life with an extremely domineering, sarcastic, moody man.

Madeleine's marriage to a man with latent homosexual tendencies dragged on for almost 15 years.

The breakdown was complex. After three years I took a job elsewhere and commuted back at weekends, thus disguising the rift and making it tolerable. Two years later I lived on my own; his illness brought me back. Eventually we both formed other relationships . . . We twice attempted a reconciliation. The same recurrence of his lukewarmness and lack of interest in me or my life or in the physical aspect of marriage made it most unrewarding.

And Veronica's marriage lasted for 19 years until she could stand no more.

He was possessive, contrary, made all the decisions, awkward, clumsy socially, never wrong. I tried throughout the marriage to discuss these difficulties, more so in later years, but was not believed and was accused of imagining everything. The children growing up and leaving made me realise I could not bear to stay alone with him for the rest of my life. Two affairs with adult men heightened my awareness even more of my husband's immaturity. He responded badly to the separation, and verged on a mental breakdown.

Harriet's marriage, although based on a warm and friendly relationship, was dogged by sexual problems which gradually worsened.

We tried a sexual dysfunction clinic, but saw a very amateurish inexperienced woman who got nowhere near us. It made things worse. By that time we had settled into a brother/sister relationship. I found it more and more impossible to live without an ordinary sex life. We were both involved with other people and it was all too stressful and upsetting. Finally my husband agreed to move out. We have talked about reconciliation and stayed friends, but getting back together does not seem possible.

Harry finally found the excuse he needed to walk out:

> Although I was still living with my first wife, we tacitly accepted that the marriage had broken down years before. At 5.30 I used to go to the pub for a few hours, take the car home just before 9 to pick up my push-bike to go to the pub for the evening. Some nights I never even went indoors. It was just a place to go with people. I met Rhoda at work and was immediately attracted to her. After a few months I asked her to come with me on a business trip to Scotland and she agreed. When we went I made a conscious decision that whatever happened I wasn't going back. I told my wife I'd reached the point of no return. Taking Rhoda away was almost an excuse to get out of the situation.

Even for the partner who instigated the separation, and whose primary feeling may be one of relief, there's still a large helping of guilt, sorrow, grief, anger and sometimes doubt. Charlotte put up with five years of violence before eventually achieving a prolonged and difficult divorce.

> My arm got broken when he was knocking me about. I left him again then. But he begged me to come back and I said I would on condition nothing like that happened again. That was in April and I think in my mind it had finished then, I didn't put the effort into it any more. The violence happened again in December and then I started the divorce proceedings. I couldn't move out because I worked from home and had nowhere to go. We lived in separate rooms. I used to barricade myself in, and once he broke the door down. That went on for 10 months and by the end of it I was a wreck. I had this

terrible hang-up that I was divorcing him because he was an alcoholic, which is an illness, and if he'd had a disease like cancer I wouldn't have left him.

Kate's marriage broke down through her boredom, but nonetheless was an exceedingly sad ending for her and a bitter loss for him.

I got restless. He was 10 years older and quite content to sit in his armchair in the evenings, watching TV and being boringly married. One day I said I want to go abroad for a long time, are you coming? He agreed to travel for a few months, just to get it out of my system. But it didn't work out that way at all. Having got a taste of the Mediterranean and travelling, I wanted more. But he'd found it hard to adjust to being abroad . . . He decided to come home and said to me 'Come back when you're ready.' We said goodbye at Barcelona station. I felt dreadful when he left because he'd been my father figure and my support. I was appalled, it was shattering. I think he thought I would go back. We wrote to each other and he was very supportive. And when I did come back to England after almost two years I sent him a postcard and he appeared immediately with a large bunch of roses, assuming that we would take up where we left off. But you can't turn the clock back and everything was different. We did stay friends from a distance I suppose, but he took a long time to accept it. We didn't get a divorce for ages, until I was living with someone else and had had a baby. Even then he came to see me and asked me to come back and said he'd take the baby, he didn't mind. He hung around for ages which I felt very guilty about . . .

Alan says his marital problems,

could be the subject of an essay. I felt she didn't want to go out in the evening after my hard day's work. She'd had a hard day as well, with two small children, and she was unwell. But I'd become inured to her complaints and didn't take them seriously. We discussed our difficulties only at crisis point. Why? Because I'm not very good at discussing such things and I suspect she was no better. I had violent tempers but never hit her. The furniture suffered. She was non-violent to the point of irritating passivity . . . The breakdown happened gradually. I was unfaithful on three occasions and she found someone else and told me I had to go. I was devastated, full of guilt and anger. I realise now that I never understood my wife on an emotional level, and I still don't.

Laura sought help through the Marriage Guidance Council in her first marriage before giving up.

It helped me to acknowledge the decision I'd already reached, i.e. to part. In the first instance it hadn't occurred to me that I could end it — marriage was 'for ever'. My husband was greatly offended by my decision. He cut the housekeeping money to a bare minimum and in the last two months to nil. His influence on the children was very damaging as he told them to take no notice of me (knowing that I was to have sole custody) and that I spoke a lot of rubbish.

Geoff's marriage deteriorated over a period of years, but he left his wife very suddenly.

An old attachment existed between my wife and another man which was re-awakened on their meeting again. My wife then ceased to show the same interest in my pursuits. We sought outside help, but it was no benefit because it could not solve the problem of her other man. The realisation was gradual for me, but the decision to walk out was sudden. My feeling on separating was devastation — a complete void. My wife I suspect reacted with feelings of extreme guilt. She married the man in question.

IRRETRIEVABLE BREAKDOWN

Rachel's marriage was undermined by problems with her stepson and the relationship was strained to breaking point when the couple moved to Israel.

We didn't have a single idea in common about what we wanted our lives to be like. I got no support from Sam over anything. He wouldn't help me learn the language, was too busy to help with any of the bureaucratic procedure of getting established in the country. He started keeping very irregular hours, and wouldn't have a phone installed. He used to come back late, unpredictably, and was always putting me in the wrong. I think by then he was having an affair. Then I met my parents for a holiday and realised that when I got away from him I felt totally liberated. Soon after that I came back to England to visit my sister and I spent three days crying and talking, crying and talking, by the end of which I'd made the decision to leave him.

For a partner who resisted the break, or to whom it came like a bolt from the blue, the blow to self-esteem and confidence, and the depth of bereavement and loss can be colossal. Helen's marriage lasted for 12 years, with any frictions unexpressed, and then collapsed with terrifying rapidity.

I only recognised problems in the last 12 months when he went into mid-life crisis identity problems. I never acknowledge potential areas of conflict — head firmly in the sand and wanting to believe everything was and would always be all right. Put simply, my husband began acting like an adolescent and fell for a 17-year-old girl he was teaching. I was panic-stricken and totally demoralised, very jealous, very unhappy. It never occurred to me that I had any power to influence him, just that he wanted someone younger and that I had lost him for ever. The marriage disintegrated over about six weeks. I was breaking down and a psychiatrist saw me and suggested I and my children move in with my current partner. I'd met him only three months earlier on a 'personal growth' weekend, to which both of us had been encouraged to go by our spouses. His marriage had also recently broken down. After about a month my husband asked me to return, but I felt committed to my new partner so we divorced immediately. Angry feelings predominated, having been suppressed throughout marriage. I remained confused, exhausted and near breakdown for a long time.

Diana's marriage breakdown was slower but no less shattering.

I developed anorexia as a follow-on to postnatal depression. He became more aggressive, and eventually found someone else. I asked him to leave via a solicitor's letter. My husband was very bitter, and used the children to get at me. He tried to frighten me and threatened me. He now lives with a young girlfriend he had while we were married.

Maggie tried hard to save her marriage and was appalled when her husband finally left her.

We had endless cul-de-sac discussions over the jealousy thing, but they seemed only to exacerbate the problem. He ended up even jealous of my relationships with my immediate family. All our discussions were focussed on him. Once, when we were facing the end of the marriage, I threw my straw slippers at him in frustration. They were so light that they didn't cross the room. But the angry gesture touched off an untypically violent reaction. He tried to break a pile of plates over my head . . . I made efforts at reconciliation before we were divorced, but gave up because he was completely focussed on his second wife. He said things like 'I don't love you and I never have' — untrue, but very daunting. My world was shattered when we separated. I felt terrible bereavement. I was defiled, rejected, soul-lonely, sometimes I didn't know how to get through the day, even the next few minutes.

What a catalogue of misery and misunderstanding, grief and sorrow. No wonder that it can take months or even years after a separation to feel half-human again, and able to tackle the world. But the time after a marriage ends need not just be a time of loss. It can be an opportunity for reappraisal and adjustment, a time to absorb what has happened and come to terms with it; a chance to assess priorities and prepare for a different and better future.

3. BETWEEN THE ACTS

Getting over the separation, adjusting to life alone, preparing for the future

Separation is only the beginning. After the parting, when the dust starts to settle and life gets back to some semblance of normality, many people find themselves in a world that's altered beyond recognition. Some start rebuilding their lives straight away, others sink into apathy and depression from which they may not emerge for many months. For some, the level of loss is equivalent to that of a bereavement, with the additional anguish of coming to terms with the rejection implied by their partner's continued separate existence. Everyone reacts differently, but the period immediately after separation is generally remembered as a disturbing time, if not always entirely unpleasant.

THE BEGINNINGS OF ADJUSTMENT

Although some people make the transition to singledom fairly smoothly, many go through a phase of switchback emotions, from relief to sadness and back again. They may act strangely, their ability to make decisions may be impaired, they may have trouble sleeping, lose their appetite and concentration, and generally feel disorientated.

Rachel had been abroad for three years with her

husband when her marriage ended, and found herself totally disoriented.

When I first came back, I was in a very peculiar state. My metabolic rate was about five times what it is normally. I was really speedy, couldn't sleep, couldn't read. I decided to get a job quickly to give a structure to my day, I didn't care what I did, so I went to the Job Shop and they offered me work as a British Rail clerk. And in all its horribleness, that brought me back to earth again.

Sue, who left her husband after years of frustration at his unwillingness to acknowledge their problems, was surprised by how bad she felt after the split.

I was filled with an acutely painful sense of loss, yet at the same time I felt immensely relieved, as if a huge rock had been lifted from my heart. It was a physical sensation as much as a mental one. I was in a state of almost euphoric joy at times, yet for three months not a day went by when I didn't find myself crying.
    At first I had nowhere to live, so I camped out with friends and family, looked at grotty bedsits and eventually found one that would do. I was very homesick for my house, garden, cats and so on. I remember eating strange meals at odd times of day. And I frequently got drunk on my own or with friends. Wine was a good prop for a while, although I didn't need it so much after six months or so, as the pain became duller. Things improved when I rented a flat from a friend who was going abroad.
    In the beginning my husband used to follow me and would approach me in the street and try to persuade me to come back — terribly upsetting for both of us. He persisted on and off for months. When I eventually went back to our house to collect some belongings I was shocked by the signs of total neglect. He must have gone to pieces for more than a year. But in the end he did

come out on the other side and started to rebuild his life.

For the first year or so my emotions were all at sea, one minute up in the clouds, the next back in the abyss. What kept me going was my certainty that I had made the right decision. And as time went by I did start to feel more stable and much happier about my life and my future.

Maggie, whose sense of loss when her husband left her was all-engulfing, nonetheless found the strength to take her life in hand.

After the separation I got a job, took A-levels and got a place at university. I took lovers. All of these helped, but it was very, very difficult to adjust. The hardest thing was being without someone to whom I was primarily important, having no one to be wrapped around (I don't mean sex). But I did take pleasure in learning to be alone for a limited time, and in finding that I was an effective, independent person.

Alan was less successful in his attempt to avoid the emotional after-effects of his divorce.

At first I missed my wife... Then I went to work in Lebanon. The adjustment there was to murder, atrocity, arrogance, desolation: being single paled into insignificance. I briefly and disastrously married a Lebanese: motives were my own guilt about marriage no. 1, pity, a desire to help someone in a desperate situation, an ill-conceived wish for an element of domestic stability.

PROBLEMS FOR PARENTS

Parents have very special problems to face, because, after divorce, they find themselves either trying to cope with children alone, or adjusting to a life in which they are separated from their children. Both situations can be difficult and painful.

When Judith kicked out her philandering husband, she was relieved, but lonely and very hard up, as she found herself struggling to manage with two children. Separation for Jenny meant an even greater loss of independence than she'd suffered in a marriage that had made her feel trapped: 'I took my daughter and moved back with my mother, who reverted to her previous dominant role. I felt very angry about my life.'

Becoming a single parent in a community where you have previously been established as part of a couple can be tricky. For Harriet:

> Social relationships were difficult — I didn't want to be with couples any more, and didn't know many single people. I stayed in the marital home and, as I am a parent, life was similar, though I did feel empty in the evenings and lonely at night. I took in lodgers which helped a bit with money and company, except they tended to drink my gin, run off without paying or try and seduce me. The hardest thing was being responsible for everything, having no one to help with home/child, the constant drudgery of organisation.

Laura felt the reverberations of her separation mainly through her children.

> The relief of leaving was great, but I felt very guilty about the effect on the children although I knew it was for the best for them. Things improved once my ex stopped seeing them. It was easy to adjust — I had the boys and friends dropped in continuously. I took out a mortgage to buy a house which was a financial struggle at first, but I coped.

Lynn, who had been afraid she would not be able to cope alone, found that the reality wasn't as bad as she'd feared.

> When we first separated I did wonder what I'd done, and how I would cope bringing up two children by

myself and managing financially. And I wondered too if I would still have my friends and how they would treat us now we were not together. But once I set my mind to it and admitted 'This is it, get on with it the best you can', the relief was unbelievable. Being alone didn't worry me really, I'd got so used to it with my husband being away a lot on business and often out.

Adjustment was harder for Geoff, forced to leave his sons behind with his ex-wife and her new partner. 'It wasn't easy to adjust to not being responsible for others. I was living in digs for two years, which didn't help. The hardest aspect was not being really close to anybody, not needing to consult anyone else in making personal decisions.'

Michael also regretted leaving his children, but after having an affair and falling deeply in love for the first time in his life, he realised just how much the relationship with his wife lacked and, after much agonising and attempts at compromise, he decided he could no longer live under the same roof with her. 'When I told her I was really going she ran away for four days and did not tell anyone where she had gone. I felt liberated when I left, but even though I saw the children often I still missed them, and the mess of family life, terribly.'

FACING THE FACTS

Coming to terms with the end of a marriage means facing head on everything that has gone wrong. Charlotte had felt guilty at leaving her violent, alcoholic husband. But what she discovered after the separation changed the situation.

If I'd known he'd been unfaithful the whole thing would have been much easier because I couldn't have forgiven that. As it was I always felt guilty because I hadn't done much to help him cure his drink problem. The day before I moved out he said to me: 'Whatever I've done to you, I've never been unfaithful.' But later someone told me that he'd had lots of affairs. So I tackled him and he admitted it. I made him tell me everything then, because I needed to know it all and then close the door. Doing that was extremely painful, but it also made me very angry and in that way helped me to get over the break-up.

A BACKWARD STEP

The partner who does the leaving generally has to abandon the family home, and along with it may lose his or her place on the housing ladder which can never be regained. For Hilary, leaving her husband meant leaving the home she'd had for more than 20 years. 'I had no money and no roof, so I took a job looking after a married couple, both doctors, and their family. It wasn't until my divorce finally came through some years later that I was able to buy a small house.' Going back to being a tenant was one of the biggest bugbears for Madeleine. 'I like having a fixed home and did not like living in rented accommodation and considering the requirements of landlords. I looked forward to the security of property-owning again.'

Returning to the life led before marriage can seem depressingly retrogressive. Joanne had married partly to escape the hassle of single life in London, and had mixed feelings when she found herself back on the same circuit.

> As soon as I had got rid of him I felt relieved and more settled. I stayed in the flat we had shared and led the life I had lived before we met, seeing the same friends and doing the same things. I found the weekends very long, unless I arranged something definite, but I liked being able to please myself in what I did without worrying about whether he'd appear or not, and what mood he'd be in.

BRICKBATS AND BOUQUETS

Ending a marriage means ending a whole way of life. Everything changes, and not always for the better. Friends who were previously welcoming sometimes feel positively threatened. Perhaps they secretly envy your freedom, or are afraid to probe too deeply into their own marital difficulties. 'The husband of one couple tried to persuade me to have a reconciliation,' remembered Veronica. 'Then he and his wife told me independently they wished they had the courage to do what I had done.' Perhaps people feel insecure, as if separation were catching. 'Many people were censorious, all were surprised and shocked, many clearly felt threatened,' said Helen. 'Some friendships did not survive.' Diana found: 'It was as if people felt I had something contagious and avoided me. I stayed in the marital home, but missed adult company. I feel as if I have never been able to like myself or my own company.' Friends might even fear that you'll snaffle their partner: divorced women in particular are still sometimes regarded with suspicion by their married female acquaintances.

The best friends are those who don't offer an opinion unless asked, who don't assassinate your ex's character, but will listen patiently while you do, and who are there offering sympathy and support until you're over the worst. They may not be the ones you expected to rise to the occasion, but they are well worth seeking out because they can help you through the obsessive stage and back into the real world.

Some unfortunates never achieve this vital transition, and remain locked in their misery. Five, 10, even 20 years after the event they are still telling every passing stranger bitterly about their divorce within minutes of meeting. They're unlikely to find what they most desire, a new partner, until they tackle the root of their grief, a process which may require professional help if left for too long. But the majority find that the wounds do start to heal eventually, and sooner or later feel ready to take up the reins of life again. Along the way, unthinking or insensitive comments about your situation can knock you back severely. Negative reactions from family, friends, colleagues can make or break your ability to cope, especially when you're having a bad day.

Most people find they are greeted with a mixture of reactions, and the positive ones go a long way towards making condemnation, hostility or total incomprehension easier to deal with. Wendy was 'considered a wicked woman by some — extraordinarily brave by others'. For Alan: 'My own family was very supportive, although separation/divorce were alien to their ways. One old friend commented afterwards that my ex-wife had never been very supportive and was cold. I'd not really seen it that way. Madeleine had to cope with, 'one appallingly condemnatory reaction from a colleague. Otherwise people reacted with great understanding and even, from close friends, positive encouragement that we had done the right thing.' When she left her husband, Kate's mother's reaction was 'I told you so':

> We didn't talk about it a lot. I refused to. She said much the same years later when I left my second husband, but I had had such a hard time, that she was also relieved that it was over and I'd got the kids away from him because everyone was worried about them.

The end of a long marriage is often harder for people to accept, as Maggie found when her husband left her after 10 years. 'People reacted with shock. We were seen as an ideal couple and were the first of our generation to separate.' It caused a local furore when Eleanor left her husband for another man. 'My mother was angry and upset, but after much difficult discussion she finally accepted the situation. My sister was disgusted and angry. Friends were supportive. Neighbours shocked.'

Parents often surprise their offspring by coming up trumps in a crisis. Sophie's father

> had always taken the line 'you've made your bed and

now you'll lie on it', until I actually left my husband. Then he and my mum couldn't have been better — they rose to the occasion brilliantly, gave me all the help I needed, listened endlessly. And it emerged that they'd never been that keen on Danny. Some friends were a bit strange and didn't know quite how to react or what to say, as if someone had died. But others were marvellous — I don't know how I'd have got through it without them.

Happy are the newly separated who endure few, or no, direct criticisms. 'Everyone was very supportive, many couldn't understand how I'd stood him that long, including his friends,' said Laura. Russell: 'old friends were sympathetic and my parents came to accept that it was for the best. I have also remained good friends with many people who were originally her friends but who decided to discontinue the friendship with her.' Rachel was warmly welcomed back to her close-knit circle. 'My friends were upset about what I'd been through, but pleased I was back in the country, and so were my family. My parents were amazingly supportive and sensitive. They're better in a crisis than in real life!' All through her long-drawn out divorce Charlotte's family had stood by her. 'My family were delighted when it was finally over. My mother was terrified when the divorce was thrown out of court first time round that I would change my mind and not go through with it. She'd never liked him.'

NEW-FOUND FREEDOM — A MIXED BLESSING

Many people find it hard to come to terms with their new single status. A separated or divorced person suddenly has a different role to play in society from one who is identified as half of a married couple. Admitting to being divorced can be surprisingly hard. The words 'I'm divorced/separated' can stick in your throat, especially knowing how they alter others' perceptions of you. Both women and men report difficulties with their social lives once they are single again. 'Being a woman alone was very limiting to social events,' said Lynn; and Madeleine found, 'I have excellent friends, so was seldom lonely or isolated, but was surprised to discover how much I disliked a socially anomalous status.' Sue was saddened when, 'Some couples who'd invited us before stopped inviting me. But none of the people I really cared about would have done that.' And Malcolm found his horizons limited because: 'I didn't enjoy going to concerts or the cinema by myself, and couldn't always find someone who was willing to accompany me.'

Unless you have a wide network of friends, or are happy to go out alone, there are bound to be times when you feel unable or unwilling to go to the theatre, say, or on holiday, because there's no one to go with. But there are ways round the problem, which generally eases with time as your new social circle widens and you meet other people in the same position. And for those who divorced willingly, hankering after freedom, there's a wonderful opportunity to spread their wings and enjoy themselves. Sophie felt,

> quite intoxicated with the freedom, especially when I got a car of my own, I could go anywhere I liked, whenever I felt like it, and I didn't have to tell anyone what I was up to. I even got a kick out of driving down to the local shopping centre in my car, buying the food I fancied, popping into Habitat for a quick impulse buy and then driving back with the windows open, a tape playing, to have a glass of wine and lie about in my garden. I still get a buzz from that sense of total independence, even now.

Hand in hand with that delicious freedom inevitably comes a degree of loneliness. Adjusting to solitude when you've been used to having someone around most of the time may be very hard, the silence and lack of contact intolerable, to be avoided at all costs. Yet some people find a strange solace in enduring, and even enjoying, loneliness. It seems to be a very necessary part of the whole experience for them. 'For the first year I couldn't tolerate being alone,' said David.

I always kept the radio or TV on for company, and I sought out other people at every opportunity. But gradually I became used to it, and after another year reached the stage where I used to crave silence, and could spend hours alone without being bothered by it. I started to go for quality rather than quantity in my social life, and enjoyed it much more as a result.

Loneliness had a peculiar delight of its own for Kate.

After my second marriage broke up I camped with friends for a while before I found a flat. It was a difficult year, but I enjoyed it really. I loved the tramping around, liked the insecurity of it. I did worry about the children, though, as my son was sitting his O-levels and needed space to study. So he moved in with a friend to do his swotting whilst I blissfully carried on my lone existence. I'd more or less been single for years. I was very lonely, but I'd always been lonely and I'd grown used to it.

Michael's way of dealing with solitude was to compare it to his previous life. 'I was lonely, yes, very lonely sometimes. But whenever it got too bad I only had to look back at my marriage to remind myself how much worse life had been when I lived with my wife.' Rachel used the same technique to good effect.

No matter how lonely I felt, it was never so bad as the way I'd felt during my marriage. I still remember lying in bed with Sam feeling as if there was a glass partition between us and I was completely on my own. I'd had no back up and nobody to talk to who would understand. And anyway I couldn't have talked to anyone because that would have been disloyal and destructive for the marriage.

Sometimes, though, even the relief at escaping isn't enough to alleviate the pangs of solitude. Despite her euphoria at getting away from her husband, Charlotte didn't adjust easily to living alone.

I was quite proud that I had my little house and liked the independence, but I was often unhappy, mainly because I didn't like the treatment I got from men: she must be in need of a certain service because she's divorced, that sort of thing. I wanted a new man, but I couldn't be bothered with all the hassle of attracting someone, going to endless parties and always being on your own because the world is full of couples — I hated that. But I went out obsessively, and panicked if there was a white page in the diary. I didn't like being at home on my own.

Partly to combat loneliness and partly to establish a new identity, many people build up a circle of different friends at this stage, who can act as a good support network. Friends who pre-date the separation and family members can't always resist the temptation to get you safely paired up again. 'It's the old story isn't it?' said Michael.

People always want you to suffer along with them, so if they're married, they'd feel happier if you were too. Friends were always asking me if I'd 'met anyone', when the last thing I wanted at that stage was an 'involvement'. I'd have run a mile from anything faintly resembling a serious relationship.

Jenny found that 'my parents hated the idea of me being on my own, and hoped that I would remarry. And one friend in particular was always introducing me to single men, when what I really felt like was a bit of time on my own.'

PLAYING THE FIELD

Going out with different people is part of the process of establishing your new single identity and bolstering your self-confidence. Most people spend months, and often years, testing out the possibilities, whether from choice or from lack of alternatives. It is a highly instructive, if wearing , process. Geoff was on his own for 10 years before moving in with his present partner.

> I never actually lived with anyone in between, but spend short periods of time intimately with several — separately! Most relationships were of comparatively short duration except one which lasted five years and almost became a common-law marriage. I always balked at moving in with her, and the relationship eventually ended when I met my present partner and realised that she was someone I really did want to live with.

After separating, Harriet continued to see two long-term boyfriends with whom she'd had affairs during her marriage.

> Neither of these relationships seemed adequate without my husband in the background. Although I was deeply emotionally involved with both men concerned, neither of them seemed quite right, and when it came to making a commitment somehow it never came to anything. I also had a couple of 'temps' but no one who I thought remotely promising. I finally split with the two long-termers six months and one month respectively before meeting my present partner.

Many people make up for lost time by having a fling of some sort. It might involve a promiscuous phase, or be an experiment in mixing with people who have excitingly different lifestyles from the old familiar one. A time like this can be fun, or it can be disturbing. With a bit of luck it can also help you to sort out what you want next from life. Rachel's 'fling' lasted for most of the five years she was alone. A succession of male characters moved in and out of her life, none of whom made her happy for long. Eventually things changed when she got her priorities sorted out.

> There was a short, sharp affair with someone I got very attached to, without realising that he slept with anyone who came along. I was pretty pissed off about that afterwards because it was very soon after my divorce and I didn't need it. Then there was a short-lived fling with a married man whom I'd been madly in love with as a 14-year-old. I bumped into him and all the 14-year-old-feelings came back. He'd have been prepared to have quick nooky when no one was looking, but that wasn't what I was after. Then there was a rather difficult time with a man I was quite keen on. He was a loner, very much his own person, and his relationships with women were on those terms. You either fitted in or you didn't. It was upsetting because I wanted more from that relationship, but he didn't want to get involved. I carried on making the same terrible mistakes about men for a long time. I got mixed up with people who were quite happy to sleep with me but didn't want to get involved because that would have demanded something else from them. Funnily enough, a turning point came when I took up the guitar. It was difficult and challenging, and made me feel much more confident about myself and what I wanted. At that time I wasn't going out with anybody and I think now I was assimilating things, learning about myself and my potential. I made a decision that I had to do what I wanted to do. If I met somebody through that, all well and good, but meeting my needs had to be the starting point.

Laura enjoyed meeting different men after her divorce, but took care to keep her emotions in check.

For the first two years I had the fling I never had as a teenager — never got too involved, lots of boyfriends, lots of fun. Then I had two or three longer relationships hurting one man in particular who wouldn't take no for an answer, and decided I was better off on my own.

Malcolm kept himself unattached, but only just, for the 10 years before he met his present partner.

I moved in with one woman for 18 months in the middle. But I always kept my own flat, and when eventually I decided to leave York and work in London, I didn't ask her to come with me. Apart from that I had a variety of sexual and friendly relationships, about 15 partners in all, several of whom I am still friendly with. One of these relationships resulted in a child, whom I support, although the affair between his mother and me was coming to an end when he was conceived and we split up permanently soon after he was born.

During Maggie's eight-year 'gap' she explored territory which is familiar to many single women.

I had a number of affairs with men who were married. I was involved with all of them, in that I had loving feelings towards them, but had no expectations that the relationships would continue because they were already married. When I got to university as a mature student I had a three-year-relationship with a man 15 years younger than me. Again, because of the age gap, marriage was not really on (although I had great difficulty in hanging on to that).

Kate, having made a disastrous second marriage, had changed her attitude significantly by the time she found herself alone again.

I was 41 when I left my second husband and I remember thinking it was a bloody silly thing to do at

41, leave a marriage with two teenage children, two mattresses and nothing else. There have been a few men, but no one serious. It is very difficult to meet eligible men at my age. They're all divorced and wanting to whinge about it; unhappy, about to be divorced and wanting to whinge about it; or married.

IS RECOVERY POSSIBLE?

The notion that people can recover from a divorce as they would from a bout of measles is widely held, particularly among people who have not been divorced. 'Two years' is often bandied about as the time it takes to 'get over' a divorce, but among the majority of people, two years is a bare minimum before they begin to feel less raw. A few could claim immediate or very speedy recovery, the rest cite periods ranging to infinity. For some the feeling that they are on the mend occurs when life takes a turn for the better and becomes more stable. Others find the healing more gradual, progressing slowly over a long period. And for yet others it's a continuous process which they never expect to complete.

Jenny: 'It was perhaps a month before I felt I had recovered.' Judith: 'Emotionally it was a couple of weeks, financially a couple of years.' Geoff: 'It was about two years before I felt better and it coincided with getting a home of my own.' Harriet: 'I'm not over it even now, and it's three years since we split up.' Veronica: 'My children were disunited by our separation and recovery only happened when they became a family again. It took three years to sort this out.' Laura: 'Difficult to know how long it took as the relief was so great, but years certainly, not months.' Alan: 'I didn't really feel whole again until I met my present wife, four and a half years after separating.' Sue: 'I'll never totally recover, although I am finding it easier to come to terms with what happened. It's been six years now, but I still sometimes feel sad because of it, and think about it frequently. But that's not necessarily a bad thing.' Madeleine: 'I doubt that one ever fully recovers, but I do not intend to let one major failure ruin my life. Regrowth is my aim.' Joanne: 'I don't think you can ever fully get over an experience like that.' Tom: 'I don't feel yet that I have recovered, even after 12 years. There are still times when memories of the first marriage and the separation come back and are acutely painful.' Maggie: 'I still feel unhappy that I am completely cut off from my first husband, and we were divorced over 25 years ago.'

GOING THROUGH THE FORMALITIES

It's easy to talk about separation and divorce as if they were one and the same thing. Some people may think of themselves as 'divorced' from the moment they and their spouse start to live apart; or they may view separation as just the first step along the road in divorce proceedings.

Harriet and Tim live together but are still married to their ex-spouses.

> Tim's been separated for five years and I don't know why he hasn't divorced. I suspect a mixture of apathy and a residual need for security, along with a reluctance on both sides to settle property/finance and put themselves through all that. I still think of myself as basically attached to someone else. I suspect I always will a bit, even if we do get divorced. This has to be worked at, it takes time.

Filing for the divorce, with all its attendant traumas, and finally acquiring the vital piece of paper, are painful experiences.

Kate felt nothing but relief when she escaped from her second husband, but still found the divorce itself upsetting.

> We both had to go to court together to make the arrangements for access to the children. It seemed ludicrous for us both to be sitting there in front of the magistrate when my husband had had nothing to do

with the children for three years, and had hardly spoken to them in that time. He found it all very distressing and started to cry. When it was over I'd have left straight away, but he came up to me on the court steps and insisted on hugging me and wishing me well, which of course meant that I got upset as well. It was all most unpleasant and unnecessary.

The impersonal bureaucracy and pointless probing of the law were the worst parts for Sophie.

I opted for a do-it-yourself divorce since there were no children or property to be sorted out. I got the forms from the court, but I couldn't bring myself to look at them for weeks. Then one day I sat down to fill them in. I couldn't believe that I was expected to summarise in a paragraph what had gone wrong, even though I was using grounds of two years' separation with consent. How could I summarise nine years of marriage in one paragraph? And more to the point, why should I? I got really irate about it, and checked with a solicitor to see if I had to do it. And she said that I did, and what's more I had to make it something fairly unpleasant otherwise the court might throw the divorce out. The whole process was insulting and demeaning, ending when I got the decree, which was just a tatty photocopy telling me that my marriage was over. I still feel angry when I think about it. How could they reduce two people's lives and sadnesses and incompatibilities to that?

4. JUMPING IN AGAIN

The start of a new long-term relationship

Marriages have a life of their own, and refuse to lie down and die just because they're declared officially defunct by the divorce court. With time they lose some of their power and presence, but you can't perform a merciful act of euthanasia on a marriage, it has to fade in its own time. Not until that begins to happen are people freed to move forward into the next phase. Life, however, is seldom neat, and the next item on the agenda may not wait obediently in the wings until the participants are in a fit state to deal with it. Allowing time to 'recover' makes sense, but many people nonetheless find themselves getting involved in new relationships well before they are fighting fit again.

DOVETAILING

While many do not have the emotional wherewithal on tap to make a success of a relationship that overlaps the last one, for some, the only thing that gets them out of a bad marriage is having the next partner lined up waiting. Certainly people do do it and make it work.

It's easy to see the attraction of dovetailing. Going from a dud relationship straight into the arms of a new and loving partner must seem like a marvellous solution: no loneliness, close support through the trauma of separation, no wondering what the future holds in store. Eleanor, who deliberated long and hard before leaving her husband for another man found it 'very easy to adjust, I didn't need to recover because I left a miserable situation for a new and happy one. It was an exciting adventure'. And for Harry, unhappy throughout his 17-year marriage, 'having Rhoda to move in with finally prompted me to leave my wife. I'd never fancied living alone and was glad to get some domestic stability into my life.'

But swapping one relationship for another isn't always plain sailing. The situation may involve a complex web of hurts and deceptions, made more complicated when it comes to the break by battles over children. Both Wendy and her third partner were married with young children when they met.

I was a child-minder. Rick was a dad at home looking after his baby when his wife had gone back to work. We had an affair which lasted a few months. He and his wife came to dinner, Gerard and I went to them; neither of our partners suspected anything. It was very enjoyable. It was a particularly warm summer and every day Rick and I would have a picnic and spend the whole day in the park with all these naked little toddlers around us. It was absolute heaven. I remember saying to him, we'll never have such happy days as this again, because we both had someone at home earning money, a roof over our heads. In the end he told his wife about me. He was very unkind to her, he rang her at work and said I've decided we're going to have to split up and she broke down in tears. I should have known then that one day he'd do something unpleasant to me.

But then his wife did a very clever thing. She went to a solicitor who advised her to take the child because she might not otherwise get custody, having not looked after her. So she snatched the child, who was under two, and went to live with her mother.

At that point Rick asked me to move in with him and funnily enough I didn't want to. I was a bit scared. It had all been so nice and I had my own house to go back to. But I agreed. I wrote a note to my husband Gerard, just like I'd done when I left my first husband for him, saying 'Goodbye for ever', took my daughter and moved in with Rick.

It was easy to adjust, but I was right, it wasn't the carefree existence we'd had before. Soon I had to get a job because we didn't have any money. We fought the custody case, but his wife won and after that he used to go and visit his daughter regularly. That was the start of one of our biggest problems — my jealousy of his daughter — which we never solved.

REMARRIAGE ON THE REBOUND

For the majority who don't embark on a new relationship until they've had a break, the question of how long to wait between partners is a tricky one. Fate, luck or circumstance — call it what you will — has a lot to do with it, of course. New husbands or wives don't arrive to order, and some people are forced through lack of alternative to spend longer along than they would choose. In retrospect, however, those who have had a period on their own are often grateful for it, however uncomfortable it was at the time. 'I liked the sense of responsibility for my own life and was seldom lonely,' said Madeleine; and 'I know I could cope with living alone indefinitely if necessary, although I wouldn't want to,' said Mike.

For those who can't stand the loneliness or find taking full responsibility for their own lives too much of a strain, one answer is to snap up the first available new partner to come along. But think twice before you sink back with a sigh of relief, alone no more. It *is* possible to be lucky first time, but make sure you're doing it for the right reasons. Galloping insecurity and incurable loneliness are not a good foundation for a new relationship. Helen moved in with another man immediately after a very traumatic marriage breakdown because she couldn't face life on her own. She doubts now whether it was a good idea.

It was appallingly difficult to adjust to moving in with

someone else. We were living in a small furnished house in a strange town with my three children aged nine, eight and six and his eldest girl, just 12. We were all trying to recreate a familiar and comfortable environment — impossible. I was still desperate for security, someone to look after me and my children. I have grown up since! It felt exceedingly dramatic and romantic at the time, though I am a conventional and timid soul and was rather appalled at what was happening, too.

And Diana fears that her second marriage will also end in divorce. She had no relationships in between separating and meeting her second husband six months later. 'The decision to marry was based on insecurity on my part, the need for a commitment and financial reasons. My family and friends had reservations about it, as they thought his children would prevent lasting happiness, and they were right.'

Hilary met her second husband as soon as she left her first, although for various reasons they didn't marry for another six years. They are now divorced.

I had many misgivings about marrying Philip. During the first few years I longed for it to happen, but gradually I realised that it would be quite a gamble. We lived together on and off and at one point I chucked him out as I felt he was using me, but a few months later we came together again; I discovered I was more miserable without him than with him. When he finally asked me to marry him we were on holiday abroad, with my daughter and his two children, the first time we had all been together. It was not working out. Philip was bad-tempered and drinking too much. We had a big row and I threatened to come home. Philip threatened to shoot himself if I didn't agree to marry him and said he would be quite different as a husband. Always a gambler, I took the plunge. The wedding was arranged in three days in hot Cypriot sunshine, and the marriage lasted five and a half years.

Kate was depressed and lonely a year after the end of her marriage. She had been abroad and returned home.

> Last time I'd lived here I'd been married and settled. A lot had happened in between, but it wasn't until I got back to England that I realised that from now on I was well and truly on my own. I met Sunny, who's Nigerian, within a year of coming back. We met in a jazz club where I was working and there he was propping up the bar, looking and sounding exotic. I'd lived alone for about a year and I didn't like it at all. I'd lost touch with friends and I was very hard up so I was working long hours. And I thought it was time I had a baby. All of which probably explains why I fell into Sunny's lap so easily. He moved in with me straight away and my son was born the following year. Sunny went along with it, I thought. But I've come to the conclusion I didn't think very much in those days.
> It was disastrous, the problems were cultural, a totally different outlook. I didn't realise the huge gulf there was between his way of looking at things and mine. Everyone had told me that it was impossible and not to do it, but that just put my back against the wall and I said I'm going to do it. And I did.

If someone has been recently left or rejected by their spouse, remarriage on the rebound is usually asking for trouble. Desperate to prove their own worth, and distraught to find themselves alone, they wed hurriedly in an attempt to salve the wounds without examining what went wrong before. Simon's story is typical and it is only now, years later, that he has gained enough self-knowledge to understand what happened.

> My wife went off sex after four or five years of marriage. I considered this to be entirely her problem and looked

to her to do something about it. She had some counselling, which I refused to attend with her, but it didn't help. I can seen now how I buried my head in the sand, but at the time I was very angry at her physical rejection of me and wouldn't face up to the possibility that my attitude to her might have had something to do with it. Things didn't improve and in the end she said she didn't love me any more and that she was moving out. I was devastated, horrified. But once I'd got over the initial shock I decided to show her that just because she didn't want me any more didn't mean no one else would. I met Sandy in a pub and married her three months later, hardly knowing her. It didn't work out, of course. I was still missing Gill, still angry at her and at all women. Sandy soon sussed out that she was just a replacement, there was a string of violent rows and after 18 months I'd had enough. This time I did the leaving, and I made up my mind not to get it wrong again. I was on my own for five years after that, and in that time I did a lot of thinking and a lot of growing up. By the time I met my third wife I was very different from the man I'd been with Gill and Sandy. Lucy and I have been together for three years now and I would say the marriage is very happy.

The chances of a swift remarriage working out are better for someone like Charlotte, who thought long and hard before giving up on her first marriage, and has remained convinced of the rightness of her divorce.

I used to see my ex-husband now and then after the divorce, and that just confirmed my view that I'd done the only thing possible. Friends introduced me to Nick less than a year after I'd separated, and I fell for him straight away. We decided to get married very quickly, after about a month and this time I felt it was completely right. I was more relaxed about it and I didn't have any reservations at all, surprisingly. I was looking for romance again and I couldn't believe how lucky I was because it was such a romantic relationship, which I loved. We've been married for three and a half years and my expectations have been fulfilled, very much so. It's been lovely.

ATTRACTION OF OPPOSITES?

Some people are drawn irresistibly to the same type again and again and are likely to find a new long-term partner who bears a startling resemblance to the first. Others react so violently against their former partner that subconsciously or not, they seek out someone who is the complete opposite. Joanna ended up loathing her first husband, and went out of her way to find someone different. She says 'the two are so unalike I couldn't begin to compare them'. Russell also went for a contrasting personality second time around: 'My present girlfriend is more independent, less demanding (especially re money), more emotionally stable. She is not Jewish either.' There's a 14-year age gap between Rhoda and Harry, while his first wife was his age: 'There's a difference in personality as well as in age. My wife was old for her age and I was young. Rhoda's attitudes are very different from hers.' Harriet's partner Tim is, 'different in almost every way from my husband, who is a cool, but funny intellectual with a consistently even temperament.' Tim is 'warm, clever, physical, sensitive, moody, perceptive and sexy'. Madeleine finds: 'My man is not at all like my first partner, either physically or in character. He is more honest and open and admits to a great deal more in the way of human feeling. He has a more pronounced sense of humour. He is intellectually much more active and challenging.'

Wendy went from one end of the spectrum to the other.

Rick was the absolute opposite of my previous husband. Partner 1: Tory, dynamic, entrepreneur, socially adept, public school education, heavy drinker, creative, initiator, manager/organiser of people, magnetic personality, reactionary, emotional, selfish, racist, sexist, unreliable, dishonest. Partner 2: communist, careful/slow/plodder, thinker, reader, shy, cockney accent, socially inept, responsive, helper, background worker, fair, upright, honest, proper, reliable, stubborn, tenacious. At first I thought he wasn't my type since he was scruffy, short and pushed a pram. But when I got to know him I found him to be the most wonderful person I'd ever met and I still feel that, even though we're separated now.

SOMETHING OLD, SOMETHING NEW

Often people find that their new partners have some qualities in common with their previous partners but there are also important differences. Maggie's first and second husbands

are alike in many ways, both forceful, opinionated, highly intelligent, strong personalities, physically attractive, charismatic, athletic, handymen, difficult, successful careers, home-loving. How they differ is that my first husband was very disturbed, which comes out in close relationships. He is capable of terrible destructive unkindness. Very self-centred. Never did anything he didn't want to do. My second husband is kind to lots of people, a loving father, good fun, a really nice man, although difficult. He's responsible, sharing. And he would have wanted my children had I been able to have them, which my first husband did not.

Helen also found many similarities between her husbands.

My second partner is very much like both myself and my first husband in that he's introverted, rather serious, highly intelligent, not close to his parents. He is a trained scientist and not religious (my first husband was a minister), though interested in moral issues. I had more in common with my first husband.

Gill's successive partners pursued the same occupation,

shared some other characteristics but had one important difference. 'Both husbands are RAF officers, both lean on me to provide a secure base. Their tastes in music, good food and wines are the same. Orderly, disciplined, not very good at fathering. The difference is that my second husband is more relaxed, less uptight.'

The similarities are often less marked, with only one or two characteristics striking a chord from the past and these amply compensated for. Mike's partners are 'the same in that both can be abrasively obstructive. Where they differ is that my second partner has a sense of humour, is intelligent, likes music, books, pictures, delights in sex.' Geoff found that both his wives were 'excellent homemakers, both conscientious about household management. My present partner is more extrovert and enjoys more activities outside the home. She's a much better communicator which makes it easier to solve any problems that may arise.' Alan's wives 'both have dark hair, both are English. Otherwise they differ totally. My wife is extrovert, happy, popular with everyone, capable and fun. My first wife was very retiring, certainly academically bright but otherwise not bright, self-conscious about her very slim figure.'

Diana's comparison is short and to the point. Here's a woman who knows how to pick a loser: 'This husband is not violent, but he also lacks any emotion.' Sophie finds more to be positive about.

> Similarities are that both of them can be domineering. Also, both tend to withdraw into themselves if there's a row or they feel hurt. They are sociable types and feel at ease in groups of people, unlike me. My second partner differs from my first in that he is perceptive, can be self-analytical, will talk far more openly about everything including his fears and feelings, is prepared to confront problems and sort them out, is very physically affectionate and loving towards me, has many interests in common with me, is interested in my life, enjoys sharing.

A COMMON EXPERIENCE

The knowledge that both have undergone the experience of divorce draws many couples together. If two partners have been through the trauma, it gives them a basic fellowship, a feeling that they understand a difficult experience that others can't fully comprehend. However, the fact that they are both carting around the emotional legacy of a divorce besides possibly having dependent children and an ex-spouse who is a very real presence, can add to major difficulties in the life of newly paired divorcees.

In fact, the majority of divorced people choose partners who have *not* been married before, but even so, they can still suffer from the problems of a history of relationships, and it may be even harder for a new partner who has not experienced divorce or marriage before to cope with these difficulties, or to understand the influence of their partner's history. Said Rachel: 'Mike hasn't been married before and I think he sometimes wonders why on earth I married Sam, and how I stuck it for so long.'

WHAT ARE YOU LOOKING FOR?

Many people have unrealistic expectations of their first marriages, or no idea of what to expect. So how do they fare next time? Do they and their prospective partners discuss in advance what each wants from the partnership, to ensure that there is sufficient accord? Do they work out their own needs, priorities and areas of compromise more thoroughly than they did all those years before? What do they want from a new relationship — and do they get it?

Some, like Hilary and Kate, both of whose second marriages ended in divorce, admit having learned little, or ignoring their better instincts. For Hilary: 'The only true thing we had in common was that we had both escaped unhappy marriages and that we had both been dominated. Strong physical attraction was what kept us together. And I was reluctant to face living alone for the first time in my life.' And Kate had set my heart on having children and as I can't think of a deeper commitment than having a man as the father of your children I thought that would be enough to make a go of it. I just assumed that we would have children together and therefore be united and it didn't cross my mind once that when the babies were here we wouldn't be joined. It was the worst thing I could ever have done because he was so jealous. His attitude to children was so different from mine and so hard. I couldn't talk to him — one didn't talk to Sunny, because he just turned his back and shut the door and left. He was never violent to me, but he was to the kids. I played piggy-in-the-middle for 15 years. I thought the children needed a father, particularly as he was foreign, and I thought it was better for them to have him around and identify with him somehow. But with hindsight I think I was wrong and it damaged them far more to stay with him.

Some 'second-timers', many of whom consider their second relationships a success, had had deep reservations about getting deeply involved again. Harriet: 'I want a commitment, but I'm finding it hard work. I expect more sex, more domestic commitment, more closeness from the relationship with someone more able to talk about his feelings. We are talking it out, haven't made a full commitment yet.' Geoff: 'I feared that we both, having lived singly, might find it difficult adjusting to living with one another. We had to respect each other's way of life, not expect agreement all the time.' His second partner, Laura, had deeper reservations, tempered by her realisation that the relationship had much to offer.

It was not at all easy to make a new commitment. I was afraid of losing my independence. Also Geoff moved from the west country to London to live with me and gave up a home and many friends. Nor did he like the idea of living in London and I felt this to be a great responsibility. We have much in common, music in particular, but also reading, the theatre, the countryside, the radio and doing things separately, not living in each others' pockets. We also enjoy being quietly at home together doing nothing in particular.

Others, having taken time to get to know their second partners and make new commitments, have been able to do so without misgivings. Maggie:

> After living with my second husband for six years, through all sorts of traumas, it felt as though marriage was the right thing to do. It wasn't difficult to make the commitment . . . I felt as though I was with someone I understood and who understood and liked me. It is pretty well a success; yes I would say the second marriage is alive and well.

And Madeleine:

> We had worked together and been great friends for nine years, for eight of those without (on my part) conscious awareness of the growth of deeper feeling. (It dawned on him a little earlier, but then I've always been slow and cautious in such things.) For eight years we were simply excellent friends and comrades. I hope this relationship will be very different in outcome, but essentially I hope for the same desirable qualities of companionship, shared enjoyment, mutual security without mutual stifling, and physical warmth and fulfilment. I was not consciously looking for a partner when this relationship began. I had already grown to value his good nature, his depth, his warmth and his intelligent sense of humour by the time we realised our deeper feelings.

Marianne comes into an unusual category: she plans to remarry her ex-husband, from whom she was divorced three years ago. The intervening years have given them both a chance to reassess their relationship and rewrite the ground rules.

We parted because neither of us was very good at acting a role and didn't want to tell the other. There was tremendous questioning at the time of ourselves and each other, great unhappiness. We've been very fortunate as we have always had a tremendous bond and it has kept us communicating. We intend to marry again at some point, but this time basing our marriage on the recognition that it is a partnership, that both partners need their own space to be free and develop, as well as cuddles and togetherness. We hope to support each other, not stifle each other, and as much as it is possible, not be affected by outside pressures.

Many people speak of being far surer of what they want from a partnership the second time, an awareness made possible only by realising what was lacking before and actively seeking to make up for that deficiency. Veronica:

I knew my present partner for many years before marriage, but not very well. He'd been married for 24 years, had two children, it hadn't been much of a marriage for many years. He'd had a number of relationships and his wife closed her eyes to these so long as she stayed married to the outside world. I knew that I wanted a real friend who had empathy with me this time. The first time round I didn't know what I wanted until I realised how much I didn't have in that marriage. A sense of humour was important too. I'd forgotten how to laugh with someone, at someone, at myself. And I wanted a rock to lean on, I was fed up with being mother to my husband and needed an adult to discuss things with. It is a success. The most difficult part has been living with someone who had no relationship with his wife for many years: they were both only children and not used to talking, but that has changed quite a lot now.

Rachel:

The first time I married I was filled with trepidation, I

felt as though it was nothing to do with me because my parents arranged the wedding. I didn't feel at all like that this time, partly because I was much older and much surer that my relationship with Mike was on a more sensible footing. We hadn't let our parents take over. Mike's mother wanted him to go home for the night before the ceremony, but we put our foot down about that. We went to the wedding in our dirty yellow car. It was much more relaxed and it was ours. I didn't want our relationship to be different after we were married from what it was before and it wasn't, because we'd decided that it wasn't going to be. This relationship seems to be built on a solid foundation and I never felt that my first marriage was. I do feel grateful for that every day. I assess what's happening in a more realistic way all the time, in a way I didn't before and feel much more able to voice my fears. I can say to Mike 'when you do such and such that makes me feel insecure because of this, that and the other.' Towards the end of the first marriage I was saying that, but Sam wasn't listening and I was screaming into a void.

Charlotte:

We just think the same way. We don't argue much, we both want a family and a home and fun together, no hassle about money, no hassle about him staying out late. We'd rather be together. In fact I try to persuade him to go out more without me. I'm not so naive now, I've learned to talk things out. My first marriage wasn't a relationship really because we didn't do anything together. If he drank too much I would try and retrieve the situation on my own because I knew if I didn't there'd be a scene. I was determined with this relationship that whatever happened we would talk things out. I do it more often than Nick; for instance, he's having problems at work at the moment, and he keeps quiet because he doesn't want to worry me. But I try and encourage him to talk because I'd rather know so that we can cope with it together.

Alan:

> My expectations were not the same at all. By now I knew the right kind of woman for me. I had even decided within a year of marriage No. 1 ending that my present wife (who was with a different partner then) was the right kind of lady for me, without any intention at the time of doing anything about it. In so far as I chose her (and not vice versa) it was because she complements me. I had no reservations since she accepted me for what I was.

TO MARRY, OR NOT TO MARRY?

Throughout this book I have seldom differentiated between couples who are married for a second time and those who are living together but unmarried. Some couples allege that there *is* no difference: marriage is just a legal procedure which they don't consider necessary. That's fine if they both feel that way, but difficult if one is keen to marry and the other reluctant. Tom: 'We have not married because we are both scared of getting tied down again.' Wendy: 'I left my husband for him and I would have liked to marry but he was definitely against it so I agreed not to.' Laura: 'We haven't married because we don't need the legal piece of paper and no children are possible.'

Others feel less happy to defy a powerful convention. Many people live together first and work up to marriage gradually. It is a big step, after all, and it seems all the bigger when you've got it wrong once. Still, only a few are put off wedlock for life by their experiences: the majority seem to find little difficulty in plucking up courage to take the plunge again. Family pressures are still fairly influential, although not as strong as for first-timers. Other reasons for marrying range from practical and financial considerations, to deeper emotional desires for commitment and stability: the commitment to each other seems deeper and more significant if it is reinforced by marriage. Madeleine comments:

> We are not yet married. We intend to be when we feel the right time has come, but not immediately after my divorce. We want to marry for all kinds of reasons. Some are practical, like travelling to Italy, a catholic country, where part of his work is; some emotional, in the sense that people interfere less between married couples; and some more complex, for instance, we feel his children will benefit from seeing a long-term relationship of marriage working well, as their parents' did not.

Harry: 'There was nothing logical that made us get married. I suppose it is a commitment to someone else, rather than just living together. Although that's totally illogical. We just did it, it was convention. Rhoda: 'No, it didn't make any difference. We weren't thinking of a family at that stage.' Rachel: 'We got married because we were fighting a lot of battles and we couldn't face another one. Because of our politics Mike was facing a lot of flak from the Jewish community. His parents were giving him a hard time and we didn't care much either way. Had we not thought about having children we wouldn't have.' Joanne: 'We'd known each other for 13 years before marriage, six of those as acquaintances. We were living together in my flat and decided to move to his flat, so this gave me legal security. It was also a public declaration of our lasting unity (we hope!). After living together for so long I didn't think it would change anything very much.' Veronica: 'It didn't really bother us one way or the other whether we married, but my children and one of his wanted us to do it.' Lynn: 'We thought it was right to marry for the sake of our children.' Kate: 'It was for financial reasons. We thought the tax situation would be better.' Alan: 'We were together for four years before marriage. We were (and still are) good friends and companions so marriage seemed the obvious thing to do, since we intended to stay together for life.'

OUTSIDE INFLUENCES

You might think that decisions about the future should come entirely from the two people concerned, and perhaps they should. As long as they can accept each other, warts and all, nothing else ought to matter. However, most people also hope for the approval of others close to them. Because the marriage market for second-timers includes a wider range of people than they might have considered as partners before, families may have to accept differences of age, religion, culture, background and so on that would previously have been unacceptable. Children can be the harshest critics of all; parents and friends are also quick to express their reservations.

Harriet: 'Friends vary in their opinions of Tim. Those who knew my husband are comparing Tim with him. Friends I met after the split up are very enthusiastic.' Tom: 'Some friends were concerned because Sue is 14 years younger than I am. One said "I hope she doesn't want children". My kids asked her what she was doing with an "old man" like me.' Joanne: 'When I announced I was getting married again I felt nobody thought it would last. There was an atmosphere of "oh no, here we go again."' Laura: 'My father was worried about the extra responsibility I would be undertaking because of Geoff's blindness, but I was able to reassure him. My younger son was delighted, and so was the older one once he got to know Geoff — I think!' Eleanor: 'I left my first husband in order to live with my second. My sister is still very angry about the whole business and didn't attend our wedding. My mother had reservations at the beginning but is more accepting now.'

As Eleanor found, even if it takes a while, most families are surprisingly adaptable and usually come round to the idea of remarriage given time and the opportunity to understand. Madeleine:

> At first my family reacted very badly, because I had spared them the details of the decline of my marriage

and because I did not tell them of my new relationship until it was fairly certain that it was a practical proposition. Once they had worked through their understandable upset, which was in many ways founded on the provincial social proprieties they cherish, they met him, liked him and have warmly welcomed him. His close family have been exceptionally supportive to both of us and have received me warmly. His mother, with whom I have evolved a warm friendship, has expressed her pleasure that her son now has someone of his own 'stature' who genuinely cares for him and his children. At the same time she is scrupulously fair in keeping up with his ex-wife and is a devoted granny. I cannot stress enough the help which such magnanimity and generosity has given us both, and I am all the more touched in that I am a non-Jewess coming into a Jewish (although non-practising) family where the cultural dice would normally be heavily loaded against a second marriage.

FACING THE FEARS

Outside influences notwithstanding, it's what goes on between the couple that makes or breaks the second relationship. There has to be a willingness on both sides to face the possible problem areas realistically and agree on how to tackle them. Some problems are easily resolved, others are far more difficult and complex. It's tempting not to investigate these danger areas too deeply, to think, 'We'll sort that out when we're married'; 'I/he/she will change'; 'It'll be all right if we love each other enough'. Old myths. Yes, things can be sorted out; people can and do change; love helps. But only if you're willing to look the problems square in the face and tackle them together. Difficulties over stepchildren, the question of whether to start a new family, financial problems, where to live, how to manage the money, are all important areas to discuss early on. Don't overlook the emotional legacy you've both been left by the past, which can manifest itself in so many ways, from bruised self-esteem through a whole host of fears: of commitment, of losing independence, of being stifled, or not making it work. There is much that partners can do to comfort and reassure each other, given the will to succeed. These very understandable worries can be diminished by examining them rationally and talking them over calmly. Shrinking them to manageable proportions may take time and patience, but it is possible, as many second-timers have found.

Sophie and her second partner have been together for three years and are only just reaching a stage where they can look ahead confidently.

> We have talked through in great detail, over a period of many months, what we both want from our relationship. It's been difficult, frightening and sometimes painful, as we have both had to expose our deepest fears, reservations and vulnerabilities to each other, but we couldn't go on until we'd done it. Last year we almost bought a house together, then panicked at the last moment, took fright and split up for a while. The reason was that were were too many unresolved fears lurking in the backs of our minds, which neither of us had had the nerve to express. The relationship was too good to let go, though, and eventually we got back together and did a lot more talking, facing up to our possible problems. None of them are easy: they include difficulties with his teenage children, our ambivalence over whether we want to have children together, fears of losing independence or feeling crowded, plus all the usual anxieties about whether we can put up with each other's foibles. Nothing can be solved overnight, it's all much too complicated for that. At least we've recognised the difficulties, know where we stand on them, and agree that we are going to try our hardest to sort them out together as and when they arise. Having got that far, we were both ready to embark on joint property-buying again and feel much more confident about our future together.

5.
SETTING THE BOUNDARIES
Writing the rules for a successful partnership

A first marriage starts from scratch, with a blank slate. Both parties negotiate for what they want according to their preconceptions about marriage. Second time around it's different: it's now familiar territory, scattered with easily recognisable landmarks. The previous marriage may have had its lousy moments, but as a basis for day-to-day existence it had probably become almost second nature. You might think you'd forgotten all that domestic detail, but get back into a twosome and you'll soon remember whose job you reckon it is to put the rubbish out, who chooses the wallpaper, how much freedom and privacy you want for yourself and how much you're prepared to allow your partner. You've covered all this ground before. Both of you. Differently. And now it has to be renegotiated to the satisfaction of both.

Not only that, but the time in between has had its influence as well. Live alone and you soon develop little habits, learn to cope and get pleasure from coping. Now you'll have to let go of some of that fiercely won independence and embark on something different, not a repeat of the first marriage, but a new, developing relationship.

No wonder there's often a power struggle at the start. And, of course, there are numerous areas for potential conflict, the greatest of which is undoubtedly children. Problems of pre-history, which involve laying the ghost of the first marriage, are peculiar to second-timers, too.

So, adjustments have to be made to a new way of life and the pure mechanics of living together. If one strand of the fabric of everyday life *a deux* is weak, it puts additional strain on all the others which may already be stressed. Major hurts and misunderstandings crop up over things like money, housework and sex, which can undermine an otherwise good relationship. How *do* people learn to rub along together, gradually smoothing down their rough edges, and preventing the occasional sparks from causing any lasting damage?

INDEPENDENCE LOST

When independence has been gained — or regained — after the end of a relationship, it can be a very precious commodity. And the first thing to realise about living with a new partner is that it is impossible to carry on as if you were still living alone. Obvious, perhaps, but it's surprising how often people go into a new situation privately hoping to hang on to the perks of living alone; the right to come and go exactly as and when you like, no questions asked; to behave badly and be blamed by no one except yourself; to make decisions single-handed and live with the consequences. It's not possible, for in partnerships people influence each other, judge each other, try and mould each other. They may profess a belief in personal freedom, while at the same time binding each other with silken cords, tenderly clipping each other's wings. Living together needn't be a prison and can come as a welcome liberation from an overdose of going it alone. But, like it or not, part of the deal involves freedom curtailed, thoughts imposed upon, actions questioned.

Not surprisingly, the longer people have been on their own the more keenly they feel the loss of independence when they move in with new partners. Tom and Sue had both lived alone for a number of years when they met, and were in no hurry to forfeit their precious independence. It's taken them nearly three years to reach a stage where they're prepared to cohabit for real. Tom:

> We both kept our own flats through fear of getting tied down, or feeling crowded. But in fact we very quickly started spending every night together at Sue's flat and soon we were effectively living there, mainly because it was more comfortable and civilised than mine. We took a long time to make the decision to buy a shared home. We both see it as a major commitment (say it quietly!). I suspect that both of us have fears of losing independence when we actually make the move, but at the same time there's a strong nesting and bonding instinct at work.

Sue doesn't underestimate the significance of giving up her flat, even though she is looking forward to the future.

> It was getting ridiculous in my flat because it's so small. Having more space will mean we can escape from each other more easily than we can at the moment. Yet despite being at such close quarters so much of the time now, I don't feel that we really live together . . . It's still *my* flat, not ours. It's full of my things, there's no real evidence of his presence apart from a few shirts and the odd book. If I want new curtains or to have the place painted I do it without consulting him, because it's my home. I want to live with Tom, but I shan't be able to leave my lovely flat without a pang because it represents so much — my escape from my marriage, my first real taste of independence, my ability to survive and cope. I built it up as a comfortable home from nothing and I did it by myself, for myself. But I'm ready for a change now, I'm aware of the dangers of losing my independence, and I'm determined not to let that happen when we live together. When we first met we both gave up other interests to concentrate on each other. That was bad, and when we emerged from the passionate stage we'd become too interdependent. We both had to grab back a measure of independence, and

that was very hard. This time I'll carry on doing my own thing from day one. I'll see friends, keep my other interests going, and it's vital he does the same. I'm sure it makes for a healthier, less intense relationship.

Space and time to be alone and do what you want are very important in any relationship. In some ways Laura felt as if her small house had been invaded when Geoff first moved in. 'I missed having time on my own, but that has improved now. Geoff has gradually taken up various interests outside the home and now is often away for an evening or on a Saturday or Sunday, so I do get some time to myself — wonderful.'

Some people find it a relief to stop being so independent and let someone else take charge. Those who are well used to managing on their own, however, resent it when a partner comes muscling in. Judith and her second partner consider their marriage a success, but still have frequent battles over who's in control. 'I will try and take charge of everything because I always had to before. But in fact, Clive is much better at being in charge — and he'd been used to having sole responsibility as well.' And Lisa had got very used to having her house to herself, running her own life and her teenage daughter's smoothly and competently.

When Jim moved in he brought so much stuff with him. We've got rooms full of books now, not to mention his son's model race track which takes up almost the whole of the basement. Jim's job ended at about the time we met, and all the work he's had since then has come via friends of mine. It does irritate me when he's not doing anything, but still expecting me to pay the bills. I did find it hard to adjust to having someone else around the house to take notice of and look after. And he reacts differently from my husband, so my behaviour has to be adjusted. There are social adjustments too: friends, going out, different interests.

MONEY MATTERS

Traditionally taboo, money is a source of considerable wrangling between couples. Sharing money and agreeing on levels of responsibility for expenses involves honesty and, again, a giving-up of independence. For Charlotte this was one area where she was delighted to opt out when she recoupled.

> I've always been hopeless at coping with money, so it seemed natural to let Nick take over the financial side of things when we got married. The only trouble is I sometimes find I don't actually know how much we've got — not that he keeps me in the dark deliberately, I just lose touch because I'm not dealing with bills and so on myself. Sometimes I wish I was better informed about the state of our finances.

Sophie didn't object to some pooling of resources. What did make her mad was her loss of autonomy.

> When I was married we had one joint account for everything and I never thought twice about it. I wouldn't do that again. This time, we've set up a joint account solely to take care of the mortgage and bills — that was a big enough step emotionally, getting the cheque book with both names on it. Very significant. And, do you know, the bank sent it addressed to him, not both of us. I've been on my own for six years, dealing with my own finances, yet the minute I get shacked up with a man, the bank decides I don't exist, even though we are equal parties to a joint account. That TSB branch manager is going to receive a letter that's still smoking when it hits his desk.

It's easy to get used to spending how you like when you live alone, making economies as and where you see fit. That has to change when you recouple, especially if money is short. Eleanor finds that 'there's sometimes a difference in priorities, for instance my/children's clothes v. something for the house.' Even if there's agreement on spending priorities, plain and simple lack of money can be an unwelcome additional pressure at a time of great adjustment. Often in second marriages there are financial commitments from the past to be met which place a great burden on the new partners. Maggie: 'Money was a difficulty as he had an ex-wife and five children to support. Things are better now. We do have arguments about it, but they are not usually deadly.' Helen: 'Money has been scarce until very recently as the children have grown up and left home. This has only added to our endless problems.'

It can also prove difficult if not impossible to regain the financial ground lost after a divorce. Harry is still struggling to get back to where he was financially when he separated:

> I work for myself now and tend to do long hours, because I am working for money. Four years ago I left a lot behind, a big house, furniture, the lot — she kept it all. But we've not done too badly. Everything here is paid for. We've no debts apart from a mortgage . . . and I'll get rid of that eventually.

Partners' different attitudes to money can be a serious bone of contention. Lisa hasn't discussed her reservations about money with her partner, although it's obvious from what she says that they're tiptoeing through a potential minefield.

> I earn more than he does and this makes him feel a bit odd. I do feel resentful that I pay for so much more than he does, even though he is very generous with money when he has it. He doesn't contribute towards the mortgage or bills because he can't afford to, but there is also an element of my wanting to keep control, not wanting him to have a share of the house.

So far that relationship has survived and the money problems may yet be resolved if Lisa's partner starts contributing more to the household. Joanna's relationship, on the other hand, seems stuck at stalemate. After eight years she's resigned herself to her partner's reluctance to work, although things flare up now and then:

> Money has always been the main problem. He is very good at spending it, but not so good at earning it. He will not do something just to earn a living if he's not enjoying it, whereas I would. We do talk about it, but he usually starts shouting, which puts an end to the discussion. I suspect this is guilt.

Wendy's second relationship did not survive a change in her partner's attitude which she found incomprehensible and totally unreasonable.

> Around the time our second child was born Rick got involved with an ultra-left faction. He's still with them and it's horrific. He gives them all his money and all his time. People said he'd get fed up with it, but I knew he wouldn't. His convictions are pretty deep. He would give them about £20 a week; it used to make me sick. Then he had £250, a tax rebate, and he gave it to them without telling me. And later he was left £19,000 and he gave it all to them. . . . I used to rant and rave and lose my temper about it. In the end I got so angry and frustrated that I got drunk one night, lost control and attacked him. He left the next day.

HOUSEWORK: THE GREAT LEVELLER

The knotty question of who does what around the house is a time-honoured source of disagreement between couples. In second marriages the problem stems from the need for re-adjustment, in terms of what happened both in the first marriage and during a period spent alone. With honourable exceptions the stereotypes are still thriving, with many men happily relinquishing the tasks of shirt-washing, loo-cleaning and so on to women, even if they coped perfectly adequately with these chores while on their own. And women may accept responsibility for the majority of household work almost automatically, because of habits born of years of nurturing other. Others, however, dig their heels in and make a stand for a more democratic procedure. Vicky:

> In my first marriage I did all the housework, fullstop. And what's more, I felt guilty if I didn't. When I lived alone I kept my home clean and tidy, because that's the way I like it. So when I got into a second relationship I decided early on that this time it was going to be different. But it hasn't been at all easy — in fact one of the biggest rows we've ever had was about housework. We'd reached this frightfully civilised agreement about who would do what, which was fine except he never did his bit. If I said it was about time he did a bit of dusting he'd just say, later, later — and then not do it. The place was a tip and I was getting really resentful about religiously doing my share while he sat around reading the paper. We had a huge row, but couldn't really resolve it — both thought the other was being totally unreasonable. I suppose one person's dirt-tolerance is different from another's. But the problem had to be solved, so now we're looking for a cleaner to come in a couple of times a week and we'll split the cost.

Jenny's second marriage is not happy, and the couple's differing attitudes to housework are just one more element of their incompatibility. They can't talk about their problems, but it's all too easy to imagine the sort of tension that must arise in the household from her comment; 'I am aware of my own lazy attitude and my husband's obsessional traits towards housework.' Wendy's marriage was unsatisfactory, too. Her partner's lack of help with the children was a symptom of his distancing himself from the family. 'I used to sing in a choir two evenings a week, but

SETTING THE BOUNDARIES

he wouldn't look after the children properly. He was reading, writing, typing, talking on the phone and he used to ignore their cries. He wouldn't even speak to them, just shut them out. I got more and more resentful.'

Sometimes one partner is happy to do far more around the house than the other, but it takes time to thrash out the right level of involvement for both, as Geoff and Laura have found. Geoff (who is blind):

> The few arguments we have had have been caused either by my anxiety over such trivia as reaching a destination on time, or by Laura's inability to delegate in the kitchen. Without experience I cannot perform tasks perfectly and no doubt the job can be done much more quickly by her, but I end up feeling frustrated. We talk about it, though, and nothing is allowed to rankle. Also, since Laura was ill a year ago I often feel anxious in case she over-burdens herself with physical or mental exertion. She is understandably irritated by this and says she is old enough to know her limits — I must try not to be overprotective.

Laura is still struggling to break, or at least bend, the habits born of years of independence. 'I do most round the house. Geoff wants to do more and I find it difficult to let him, but continually try to let him do more. I cook, he washes up. He buys greengroceries, I buy groceries.'

The great and wondrous art of compromise, a subject which really should be taught in schools, is invaluable in dealing with these sorts of problems. Eleanor describes her husband's skill: 'We have occasional rows over his reluctance in matters domestic. He has a demanding job and I have learned to accept his non co-operation re domestic help. And he compromised — bought a dishwasher!'

People whose first partner did little to help in the house are generally thrilled to have more commitment and even enthusiasm from their second partner. Tom: 'I love the fact that she likes good food and can be bothered to cook it.' Madeleine: 'I cannot quite conceal my surprise and delight at being willingly helped in practical and household matters. It's hard to stop planning as if I were the only one responsible.' Sue: 'My first husband's cooking skills ended at the tin opener, so it's wonderful for me to have a partner who cooks a complete meal, with no fuss, no asking me what to do. And what's more, the food he cooks is absolutely delicious. We can grow plump together!'

SECOND-TIME SEX

Sex is an important ingredient of a successful relationship — there seems to be little doubt about that. It's also one of the most difficult areas in which to tackle problems. Sexual performance for both men and women is very dependent on the state of mind and can easily be adversely affected by stress or anxiety. Says Jenny: 'We have difficulty in communicating and appear to be growing further apart. Sex is not very satisfying emotionally, merely mechanical. I try to talk about this and other problems, but my husband cannot discuss them in any depth.' Helen also found that other preoccupations, not related to sex, affected the intimate side of her relationship: 'I was emotionally upset for a long while after my separation and he has suffered from depression to a greater or lesser extent for the whole of our marriage. This has had a very detrimental effect on sex.'

At the start of a new relationship, the delight of discovering each other sexually can obscure other aspects of compatibility. As the mists of passion clear, there may be nothing — or nothing desirable — left to take its place. Hilary, now divorced for a second time:

> It was sex that kept us together in the start, but once the passion burned out we were left with very little in common. There were many problems. I think one of the main ones was that we were so anxious not to be possessed or dominated by the other that in the end the very freedom we thought we had won started to slip

away. He was jealous of my children; an alcoholic, and in the end came to want a hermit-like existence, away from society. I gave up — life is too short I thought, to spend the rest of it with a depressed, irritable man who wants to spend the rest of his life in the backwoods of Cyprus. We separated three and a half years ago.

Comparisons with the ex and other previous partners are probably inevitable, even if only fleeting and unvoiced. If the comparison is unfavourable the problem can be too delicate to broach. Philippa said:

Sex was wonderful in my first marriage, it was the best thing about it, in fact. Even when everything else was terrible, we still had a marvellous sex life. My second husband is much more caring and gentler, but sexually he is less exciting and far more inhibited than my first husband.

Not surprisingly she has found it impossible to express her discontent to her second husband. No doubt he is unaware of the comparisons that are going on in his wife's head when they are making love — if he was, their sex life would probably get even worse. One ex-second-husband who did realise that he had a previous model to live up to, told me:

My wife said once how great her first husband was in bed, and that thought niggled away at my mind. I wanted to know the details — exactly what did he do that was so great? In the end I stopped making love to her because every time I'd have this image of her and her first husband in my mind and it put me off the whole thing.

VOYAGE OF DISCOVERY

Living with someone is the only way to find out the worst and best about them. Some revelations are delightful, others deeply disturbing, all require acceptance and adjustment. People even need to adjust to being happy. Veronica: 'I am never blasé and only think how fortunate I am not having to live with my first husband any more. I really appreciate what I have now. Financially I am less well off and it doesn't matter at all.' Sophie: 'He still amazes me sometimes by being so *nice*! I never expect it, always fear the worst. I suppose I'll get used to it eventually.' Wendy made an unexpected discovery about her new partner when she moved in with him. 'The first thing I learned was that he could play dozens of instruments and sing. I didn't know that about him. I've never felt like that before or since. He's got a good tone to his voice, and sitting in a room with him singing was really magic.'

There's so much to adjust to in a new relationship, so much that's unfamiliar or unexpected. Madeleine had a strange reaction to her new partner's family.

> Both my own family and that of my future husband have been extremely supportive . . . It is more surprising from my future husband's family given that, though I did not cause the failure of his marriage, I could easily be viewed as the catalyst precipitating its legal termination. In some ways I suspect that it is harder to cope with acceptance from relatives than with the expected anger and rejection, almost as if one were being denied a painful but necessary cathartic element of the process. This sounds extremely perverse, since obviously, for the most part, it is much pleasanter to receive acceptance and goodwill than unpleasantness and rejection. Obviously to each couple the whole experience feels unique simply because one doesn't encounter all the other couples out there undergoing parallel experiences in the normal course of things.

Kate had to adjust to becoming part of a different culture as well as to a difficult husband. She married a Nigerian, partly because

> the idea of dark-eyed, curly haired babies was irresistible. I did enjoy some of it — Africans are gregarious and we had a house full of Nigerians and parties and fun and we went out. I'd always been attracted to foreign ways of life, and I went bush and dressed up and learned the language and cooked the food.

Her initial enthusiasm soon waned, as her husband's attitude to the children hardened.

> Sunny thought I was quite unreasonable in my devotion to the children and babies. He was much harder than I am, the tension was horrific — I'm sure it caused my son's asthma. I knew I would leave him as soon as I had enough money to support myself and us, and as soon as the children were old enough I would go. And when they started nagging me: 'why are we still here, why do we have to put up with this?' I walked out. They were 12 and 14. Sunny and I had moved into separate parts of the house by then and he hadn't spoken to the children for months.

For Kate, the early disagreements worsened until life became intolerable. A stormy relationship isn't necessarily a forewarner of disaster, however. Adjusting can be a painful process. There is a school of thought that says that rows are a sign of adjustments being made, as each partner beats the boundaries of his or her own piece of territory. Certainly many people report rows and disagreements as being more common in the early days and not necessarily a sign of lasting disharmony. Maggie: 'Before we married, right at the very beginning of our relationship, we had a couple of punch-ups. This was very uncharacteristic of both of us. Served to clear the air, lay ghosts, etc. Certainly no violence since.' And Tom:

> In the beginning it was a repeating pattern of closeness, followed by estrangements. It happened over and over

again, but eventually it did lessen, although the old cycle still recurs occasionally. I saw it as a sign of fear and insecurity on both sides, wanting to get near, but getting scared every time we did and retreating, cooling off. To me, it was a necessary part of forging a new bond; and therefore acceptable, if unpleasant. But my partner found it very threatening and disturbing. Every time there was another distancing she felt as if everything was over, and could never believe that we would somehow retrieve our closeness.

DEALING WITH PROBLEMS

Communication, compromise, acceptance. Those are the path-smoothers, the problem solvers. Even in the happiest relationships people disagree from time to time. Perhaps more important than why they row is how they go about resolving their disagreements. Some need counselling to help them see each other's viewpoint, others shun the involvement of outside parties. A violent argument is an extreme form of communication, yet can sometimes pave the way to deeper understanding. Once again, there are no rules.

Gill:

> Our difficulties have been due to power and control struggles, resolved now mostly after 15 years of ups and downs. We dealt with them through counselling, which helped me to make changes and believe in myself. He had to change as I was changing. Talking to each other has been difficult at times.

Lynn:

> We have had lots of difficulty with the children: they against us, us against them. The wicked stepmother feeling. Half tales being told. Sometimes myself not being able to be an individual with my own ideas.

SETTING THE BOUNDARIES

Myself not being believed in taking the side of the children. We have dealt with the problems through arguments. It is very difficult when it involves the children — who believes who?

Laura:

Arguments are rare — more disagreements. We both become introverted and stop communicating but it doesn't last for long. We then talk about it and make up. Geoff is tolerant, thinking, caring, loving and fun. Our degree of irritation at each other probably measures about the same and is certainly tolerable.

Helen:

We've had endless problems, compounded by stepfamily problems. I have had to change my approach and learn to talk about problems. Marriage Guidance practice (I've now become a counsellor myself) has been very illuminating. There was some violence early on — I had to work through my fear of this. After, we both agreed it was unacceptable.

Vicky:

The nature of our problems has changed with time. At first it was all about getting used to having someone else around. Now, it's more to do with long-term decisions which affect both our lives. We used to argue furiously and neither would give any ground. These days we're much better at talking without losing our tempers. Perhaps we've got over our fears of commitment and so neither of us feels so threatened by sometimes giving in to the other.

Sophie:

We have occasional big rows, very upsetting and unpleasant. We do generally try and talk about it once we've both calmed down, although it sometimes takes a day or two before we can talk without arguing again. I don't discuss these incidents with anyone else, and nor does he. I believe that what goes on in our relationship is between us, and that we have to sort it out together as best we can.

Eleanor:

I once complained about his lack of attention towards me at a party. When we got home the whole thing escalated into a violent row and we ended up 'wrestling' on the bed. We were both very angry at each other's implied rejection. We do talk about our problems on and off and have gained in understanding of each other.

Harry:

The 14-year age difference does give rise to difficulties fitting in with a group of people. Some of hers are too young, some of mine are too old. Rhoda's nearer in age to my daughter than she is to me, which could be why she has so much difficulty in accepting Rhoda. Also Rhoda has a vile temper, and won't put up with anything and will feel very aggrieved at little things. I just let it go over my head for 10 minutes.

Rhoda:

He doesn't really have any annoying characteristics except he just won't argue with me. In some ways that's very good for me. In my previous marriage we had stand-up rows all the time, and got nowhere. With Harry, after 10 minutes I think why am I doing this, what's the point?

Veronica:

The biggest arguments were over my trying to persuade

my husband to leave his job and work for himself. He didn't really believe in himself; but he has proved to himself that he can be more successful in building up his own company which he did seven years ago. He tends to underestimate his own strengths. Similarly he has considerably supported me in my work to achieve what I never could have done without him. Since I am a big communicator I encouraged us to talk things over. It's much more natural to him now. But only children do have greater difficulties in this respect. His father died when he was four and his mother had to work hard all her life, so he grew up with no one to talk to.

UNHAPPY ENDINGS

Sad to say, for some couples no amount of attempted compromise or talk can improve things, and eventually the marriage founders. Hilary thought she knew what she wanted from a second relationship, but ended up getting the opposite.

> After my first marriage I was desperate not to be dominated. Philip had also been dominated by his first wife. We were both trying to avoid being dominated by the other, but Philip, beneath his veneer of being democratic, was chauvinistic. He had problems with alcoholism and tobacco addiction and depression. I felt I lost my freedom as his addiction got in the way of a normal life. I had to support him in so many ways — he liked me to be around all the time, but he constantly griped. My compassion was running out. He was the world's greatest hypochondriac, and enjoyed ill-health. When he was with the few people that he liked he was great fun, but the people grew fewer and fewer.
>
> It was difficult communicating with Philip. It was never easy to have a normal conversation anyway, as he was perpetually railing against the 'bloody' this and that, or some work colleague or other. He didn't want to talk about our relationship. In the September before we

broke up he got some books from the Marriage Guidance Council as I said that if things didn't improve between us I didn't think I could go on. We set a six-month period, during which time he had to stop smoking with the threat of a by-pass operation hanging over him. I suggested that we both read the books and marked the points that particularly related to our problems. Philip wasn't willing to do this. I asked him to sit down and list all the things he wanted out of marriage, the things that most annoyed him and the things he thought he could change. I was to do the same. But we never seemed to get anywhere.

Wendy believes that an element of her own character has something to do with the failure of her relationships.

Rick has changed so much; politics used to be a hobby for him before. He says it's thanks to me, because I used to encourage him to be more active. I certainly gave him a lot of confidence, helped him get a job he wouldn't have got before. I got him cleaned up. I got his hair right and his clothes right and he looks really good now, doesn't have smelly armpits. He's still a bit socially inept, but he's much better. He knows that if you go into a pub with a crowd of people you have to buy a drink, whereas before he was like a big soft teddy bear that other people told what to do.

I don't know what I feel about him now. He says he loves me, but I feel he doesn't love me enough, he doesn't love me in the way I want him to, doesn't devote his time and energies to the home and family. I think it's me, I make men like that, or I'm attracted to people who are going to be like that. I'm a bit tough and a bit aloof, I think I'm the powerful one who makes them like this. Rick never found me loving enough or affectionate enough. I was much tougher than him, he was never quite what I wanted.

Despite Wendy's 'admission', one person cannot cause

SETTING THE BOUNDARIES

a relationship to fail. It takes two people to make a relationship and two to break it. And the second time can involve even more personalities, because people from the past often have a far more important role than is admitted in directing the course of a second relationship.

6.
THE POWER OF THE PAST
Exorcising the ghost of a previous marriage

What do you do with painful memories? The natural reaction is to shut them away in some deep recess of your mind. 'Look to the future,' we're told when things go wrong, 'stop living in the past'. Yet the past has a significant bearing on the future. Old wounds have to be exposed to the air before they can heal. Of course it's important to progress, and dwelling obsessively on what has been and gone is pointless and destructive, but thinking — and talking — the past through, in order to understand and accept it, is a positive step towards building a happier and more successful relationship in the future.

It would be so easy if one could leave a broken marriage filled with healthy dislike of the ex, feeling nothing but relief that it's over. But life is seldom that simple. Although some people do come away from a broken marriage with nothing but miserable recollections and negative feelings, most have a much more mixed bag of memories. It probably wasn't all bad, and thoughts of the good times and the good side of the ex can be poignantly disturbing. The positive side of the previous marriage is hard, too, for a new partner to hear about. It's easy to listen to a tale of woe, take the side of your loved one and sympathise with his or her grievances against the ex. To hear the former partner talked about with affection,

THE POWER OF THE PAST

nostalgia or regret, is far more difficult to accept and can be very threatening.

All feelings about the ex, positive and negative, tend to recede in time if there is no contact with him or her, even if the memories do flood back strongly now and again. It's far harder to forget when children are involved, as there is every likelihood of regular contact with those people who represent so much pain.

So just how large does the past loom in the life of a new couple? As always, there's no stock answer. It all depends on the individual. There are those who can shrug off the past, or at least bury it good and deep, so that to the observer, at least, they appear unmarked by their history. Most new couples, however, take some pleasure in sharing their past experiences, especially if both are divorced. There is some comfort to be had from hearing of each other's unhappinesses and deciding that this time, together, it will be different. Most people feel the need to go through all the gory details together once or twice, perhaps over a period of months. It's part of the process of getting to know each other. But what happens next?

THE PREVIOUS PARTNER — A REAL PRESENCE

In the early years of a new marriage one or both partners may refer frequently to their ex-spouse and former marriage. How much this bothers their new partner depends very much on the terms in which these references are made. Madeleine has a good, if distant, relationship with her ex-husband. Her second partner is still struggling with the trauma of his marital breakdown.

> He often talks about it with anger that he should have been so neglected and unloved when he is essentially such a good person. I don't feel jealous. There is the inevitable painful twinge in that there are areas of experience from which I am excluded, since they involve his ex-wife's privacy too, and I quite understand that. These things just have to be taken in one's stride.

Rachel's second husband has not been married before. Even though it's nine years now since she separated, 'the past is in my consciousness. I make comparisons quite a lot and I'm often grateful that this relationship doesn't resemble that one in any slight degree. It's very hard on Mike because he's being compared with something he doesn't know about.' And Alan, who has occasional contact with his ex-wife 'when she phones to speak to her sons', says his wife 'feels a bit uncomfortable about it, but I just think how lucky I am now. My wife occasionally refers to her previous marriage. I think we're both a bit sorry for him, but it doesn't affect me emotionally.' Wendy used her second relationship as a yardstick of how much her life had improved. 'I often compared the two during the time I was with Rick, and felt happy to be with him. I was slightly jealous when he used to refer to his previous marriage, but his ex-wife has remarried now. Before she did, I sometimes feared they might get back together.'

Harriet says of Tim, who is separated from his wife: 'He talks about Helena a lot. How it affects me depends: it's good to know what it was all about; sometimes I feel, though, that the attachment is still very strong.' Diana, whose second marriage is on the rocks, claims never to think of her past, but says, 'My husband does refer to his previous marriage. He has never got over it and makes me feel compared all the time, although he denies this.'

Maggie doesn't say whether she feels compared with her husband's first wife, but she has clearly been troubled by his strong attachment to his ex. 'Now that he has managed to separate out his feelings for his first wife from necessarily living with her it doesn't affect me adversely when he refers to her. I don't mind if he loves her, as long as she realises he can't live with her and as long as he loves me and wants to live with me.'

Tom and his partner have spent hours discussing their previous marriages, which has helped give them both insight into their own relationship.

She still refers to him from time to time, but as the

references are all to his defects I am not adversely affected. I think though that she still has many positive feelings about him and memories of the good things in that partnership which she doesn't express, presumably because it's too painful. In a way I'd like her to talk about that side of her marriage, but I think I would also find it very hard to listen to.

Although a number of people claim never to think about their past life or spouse at all, for others the memories are still vivid, and are frequently re-examined — probably much more often than they would admit to their current partners. Rachel says:

There's hardly a day when I don't think about Sam or his family, or the periods we spent in Africa or Israel in some respect, even if it is fleeting. Sometimes I still get upset about it, although I don't talk about it that much. Unless people actually knew Sam they couldn't understand. I do talk to my parents about it. They need some therapeutic experience because they went through it too.

Maggie's first husband is still inhabiting her psyche, many years after their separation. 'I sometimes have dreams about him. Always the theme is our re-establishing a loving contact, but not by any means re-establishing the marriage. I do still regret having no contact with him at all. It seems unreal, after 10 years of closeness.' Sophie's ex-husband remarried recently and, although she is now happily living with her second partner, she says:

I speculate a lot about his second marriage. I wonder if he neglects her like he did me, or if she suddenly thought to herself within weeks of the wedding 'What have I done?', like I did. I'm not jealous of her — I'm far happier with my current partner than I was with him. That said, there were good times in my marriage, and I did love my ex-husband deeply for many years, so I think there will always be a great sorrow and regret for me that it didn't work.

Lingering affection for the ex probably never goes away. Harriet's marriage broke up because of insoluble sexual problems. Intellectually though, the two were well-matched and she still misses that element in her life.

I still think of myself as basically attached to someone else. I suspect that I always will a bit, whatever happens in the future. I miss my husband's consistent good humour, cheeriness and wit. Not that Tim isn't good company, but these were things I *liked* in my husband. It has only passing effects on this relationship however, which is so much better all round.

Madeleine is distantly in touch with her ex, and 'on friendly terms, so I do not agonise as I know he too is happier and wishes us well. When I do think of anything it is usually of the occasional good time rather than the bad. But obviously many of the small things of life are mute reminders.'

NATURAL CURIOSITY

Many people have a continuing curiosity about their ex which may be motivated perhaps by guilt, a desire for retribution, the need to prove something, or simply by wishing them well. People who do follow their ex's progress from a distance may decide to keep this fact from their current partner. Charlotte says:

I don't have any happy memories of my previous life. I'm very interested in what my ex-husband is doing because he blamed everything that went wrong on me. I want to know if he reacts differently now to prove to myself that it wasn't my fault. I don't tell Nick because I don't think he likes to talk about it and I think he'd be hurt.

Jim is married for the first time, but before he met his wife he lived with another woman for three years. 'Annie knows all about Sarah, but what she doesn't know is that Sarah sometimes comes into the pub where I go after work. It's nice to see her, and to catch up on what's happening — I don't bear her any ill will now. But I don't tell Annie because I think she'd feel hurt and perhaps worried by it.'

A new partner may, however, be intrigued to know more about his or her companion's ex. When you've heard every detail about these people, it's natural to be curious about them and wonder what they look and sound like, never mind more intimate speculations. If there are no children involved then the new partner is less likely to meet the old. Perhaps it's just as well. The notion of a civilised friendship between exs and current partners doesn't take into account the murky waters that have gushed under the bridge, and the depth of feeling that lurks beneath the most 'civilised' exterior. And what do you say to your partner's ex? 'I've heard *so* much about you'?

Sophie and her new partner gave themselves a nasty turn when they bumped into his ex by mistake.

> We went to see his daughter play in a concert, and the kid had neglected to mention that mum would be there too. My first reaction was to head for the door when he hissed 'That's Mary', but by then she'd spotted us. I'd often wondered about her, and it was quite a relief to find her totally unglamorous and a bit dumpy. I do have to hand it to her, though, she was very controlled, came up to us and introduced herself. It did seem very strange to be making polite small talk with this woman, when I knew the most intimate and awful things about her. I was surprised at how ordinary she seemed, to be honest. But I could see, just from that short meeting, how much he and she must have rubbed each other up the wrong way. From that point of view it was quite reassuring, since it confirmed what he'd always said, that the problem was basic incompatibility rather than there being something wrong with one of them.

Lots of people balk at meeting altogether, some meet occasionally from necessity or by accident, and even achieve quite cordial relationships. A small group appear to do the impossible, bury their various hatchets and become buddies. Judith's husband hadn't been married before, but 'we sometimes see his old girlfriends, who I like.' Joanne's husband 'is still friendly with his first wife and she has become a friend of mine. We stay at each others' houses for weekends.' And Laura too has 'a very friendly relationship with Geoff's ex-wife and family.'

Jim, on the other hand, doesn't want to meet Annie's ex-husband.

> I've got a picture of him in my mind as a belligerent little man and I'd rather not have that shattered. I've seen photos of him, so I know that really he was rather tall, and I can't imagine that Annie would marry someone belligerent. But that's not the point. I'd prefer not to know if he's a nice guy — it would make everything far too complicated. It's much easier just to think of him as a rat.

Like Jim, the majority of people find it simpler to leave a partner's past to the realms of the imagination, and let sleeping spouses lie.

INAPPROPRIATE REACTIONS

But the past can erupt in far more subtle ways than coming face to face with the ex, or making a trivial but obvious slip such as using the wrong name (which most people do occasionally). Strong feelings — anger, aggression, fear of rejection, bitterness, neediness, insecurity — can stem from childhood days and may have been reinforced by an unhappy marriage. If they haven't been allowed full expression — and most of us are taught to suppress powerful feelings which frighten or confuse us — they stay around in the psyche, waiting for a chance to leap out when they recognise one of the old triggers.

The trouble is their tendency to erupt inappropriately — as a burst of anger provoked by mild criticism; tears in the face of imagined rejection; withdrawal and coldness as a self-protection the minute there's a problem; attack as a form of defence. We behave in ways which are familiar to us because they seem comfortable and natural, even if they no longer fit the situation. We keep ourselves braced for a repeat of our former disappointments because it's too dangerous to relax and let events flow naturally.

The only way to deal with such forceful feelings is to acknowledge them, lure them out into the open and tame them. Then they lose their wild unpredictability, their capacity to frighten and confuse. But before this can be done, they have to be recognised for what they are. Annie remembers the first time she realised the power of her subconscious memories to disrupt the present. She and Jim had only known each other for a few weeks, and were away for the weekend together.

> It was around 2 a.m. and we were lying in bed, where we'd been for most of the weekend, chatting. I was just dropping off when Jim started to get friendly again. He seemed a bit half-hearted about it — we were both very tired — so I gently moved his hand and said something like, 'I'm so sleepy — let's save it for the morning, shall we?' To my amazement he snapped 'suit yourself', turned his back on me and pretended not to notice when I tried to snuggle up. It was all so stupid and quite uncharacteristic of him, but we were both exhausted and the whole thing got out of proportion. If I'd teased him, or if we'd both just fallen asleep, it would all have been forgotten by the morning.
>
> But suddenly I felt this awful misery welling up and I started to bawl my eyes out. I knew why straight away — I'd suddenly been vividly reminded of all the times right through my marriage, when my husband's turned back and obstinate silence had made me feel such a total failure, because I just could not get through to him. The frustration and rage that used to overwhelm me

then came back in full force.

Jim was a bit taken aback by the floods of tears, but once he could hear me through the sobs he soon got the picture. I was afraid he'd think I was barmy or completely overreacting but he realised that I was genuinely very upset. He even apologised for turning away from me just because his masculine pride had been temporarily wounded, and we ended up lying there giggling about it. It was such a relief to be able to talk like that. My husband simply couldn't cope with emotions — his own or mine — and would have left me to it. Next day he'd have behaved as if nothing had happened and any discussion would have been out of the question.

Since then Jim has been more careful about acting the spurned lover and I'm more aware of how and why I react to him. And we do try to talk through any misunderstandings when they happen, rather than leaving them to simmer.

Annie was lucky, because she knew at once what was troubling her and was able to talk about it there and then. A lot of people deny the phenomenon of repeated behaviour in their lives. Perhaps they have escaped it, or just don't recognise it. But many, when they put their minds to the question, can come up with examples of their own strange behaviour, which they may not recognise until it is drawn to their attention by a sometimes bewildered spouse. Rachel:

If I feel that Mike is handing over responsibility to me for things that should be shared I feel very bad very quickly. I think that's the legacy of the first relationship. It's hard on him, because you should be able to hand it over a bit. I have a very low tolerance threshold over certain things, but I always recognise it. Recently I was talking to Mike and he was preoccupied and not listening. I had this vision of Sam ignoring me, and I thought 'I can't stand another second'. I jumped up and down and yelled 'Speak to me!' I was standing near the wardrobe at the time, and since then he's called it the monster who lives in the cupboard. But he knew exactly what I was on about. I was really serious and laughing at the same time.

Veronica: 'I had a habit of talking to my first husband as if he was a child. I sometimes find myself resorting again to this manner and I hate myself for it. But it is pointed out to me!' Alan: 'My wife occasionally tells me that I don't have to behave in a particular way any more. I can't think of examples, but the thrust is that I'm treating her with circumspection more appropriate to No. 1.' Clive: 'I only get furious with my wife when she latches on to something obsessively, which was my first wife's habit.' Charlotte: 'My first husband lied to me consistently and if I ever think I'm going to be taken for a ride I overreact enormously. Sometimes, if Nick says 'We'll do this and this', I say 'Don't you dare speak to me like that.' I was so dominated before I won't let him dominate me. I know it's immature of me, but I'm frightened of being dominated because I don't want to turn back into the total little wimp I was before, not saying boo to a goose.' Joanne: 'I am told that I'm deeply untrusting, not from the point of view of sexual fidelity, but because I always fear that my husband won't keep promises, or do what he said he would do, when he said he'd do it. That must stem from my experiences with my first husband who was completely unreliable.'

Harriet likes the fact that she is forced to examine her behaviour and modify it: 'My husband would ignore any moods or bad temper, so that I could behave quite badly. I can't do that any more, as I would get a quick reaction. That's better for me, it makes me nicer I think, less selfish.'

Madeleine could only think of one 'serious' example of an inappropriate reaction: 'Though I hope I never show this outwardly. I am easily thrown if I sense something preoccupying him, an unexplained letter or telephone call for example. In fact he is so open that I always hear about everything, but my instinct is still to expect my first husband's secretiveness.'

Trivial but telling comparisons sometimes take Tom by surprise: 'It always astonishes me that my partner can read a map, since my ex-wife was a hopeless navigator. And when we've been planning things for the house, it's been second nature for me to make the decisions myself. I've had to adjust to the fact that she takes an active part, whereas my first partner was less involved.'

There is endless scope for repeated behaviour along these lines, and as a new relationship develops, new possibilities will emerge.

SUBTLE REACTION

These examples of old reactions emerging in response to a new situation are easy to understand, and fairly simple to remedy. But often the reasons for uncharacteristic behaviour are much harder to fathom. A reaction can be far more subtle than tears or irritation, say, and provoked by triggers which aren't readily recognisable. Often a sequence of events will have to be repeated many times before the reasons become apparent.

Viv, in her late twenties, had been divorced for three years when she moved in with Peter. Although the relationship was generally calm and happy, they endured months of regular rows for reasons neither understood before she realised what was going on.

> It happened whenever friends came round for a meal. I'd feel compelled to do everything myself and would start to get tense early in the evening. Usually Peter and I cooked together with no problems, but when other people were coming I tried to do it all myself and saw it as a personal failure if anything went wrong. Any contribution on his part was seen by me as 'interfering'.
>
> Not surprisingly, there was usually a row afterwards, but I could never answer his question 'Why do you act

THE POWER OF THE PAST

like this?' It didn't make any sense to me either, but I was at a loss to explain it.

Then, one day, some friends of mine came round whom I'd known during my marriage. And I found myself looking back on what life had been like then. Frankly, the memory was so painful I didn't want to think about it at all. My husband and I had very rarely entertained, for the simple, but unspoken, reason that our relationship was so shaky that it was too dangerous to risk letting anyone else near enough to notice the cracks. More than once we arranged to have people round and then had a violent — and I mean violent — row on the same day, which left us in such a state that the only thing to do was to make some excuse and cancel.

If the meal did happen, I always prepared everything myself, because that way there was less chance of trouble. It seems obvious now that those experiences explained my problems with Peter, but in fact the memories were buried so deep that I had to force myself to drag them out.

Reliving past traumas is an unpleasant experience that most people would rather avoid. Even when you do force yourself to re-examine history sufficiently to get to the bottom of a particular pattern of behaviour, it can still be very difficult to break that pattern, as Viv discovered.

We agreed that the only way to conquer the problem was to keep trying, all the time being aware of what could happen and why, and try to recognise the danger signals so that any potential upset could be nipped in the bud. Next time we were both a bit wary, but everything was fine and we cooked the meal together without a single cross word. Since then it's got much better, but I do still feel a bit nervous every time we ask people over, and occasionally the old problem does rear its head again. I think time is the only answer — you can't really expect such deeply ingrained behaviour to vanish overnight.

Although repeating patterns like these can be very painful to confront and work through, they can have a beneficial side effect, in that they encourage the two of you to talk about what is going wrong. It can take years to unravel these deep-seated patterns, and some of them may never be broken entirely. A lot of understanding is needed on both sides to do it, especially if the pattern is one which provokes anger or even violence. Jim was horrified by the strength of his reaction to Annie when she got hooked into one of her old response patterns.

She had told me that there was some violence in her first marriage, which she hadn't understood at the time. With hindsight she could see that she had often provoked a violent reaction from her husband by trying to goad him into responding to her. She felt that he ignored her problems, and wouldn't accept that there was anything wrong in their marriage. Her need to get some sort of response from him was so great that she was prepared to provoke him to anger just to prove that he had some feelings towards her.

    I understood all that, but didn't think it relevant to us because it was part of her past. And our relationship is very responsive. We are usually very aware of each other's moods and feelings and quick to react to each other. But one day we weren't seeing eye to eye at all about a problem of hers. I dug my heels in. I thought what she was doing was wrong and I said so, criticising her in no uncertain terms. Perhaps I did overdo it a bit. She became more and more wrought up because I wouldn't ease my attitude, until she grabbed my book out of my hand and tried to throw it across the room. I snatched it back and walloped her — it all happened in a second.

    Afterwards we were both very shaken and upset. Later on we talked about it, and didn't reach any conclusion. Those deep hurts and fears of rejection and condemnation will always be present in Annie, and there's something in me which goes back to my first marriage and beyond that is contemptuous of women when they show a lack of self-esteem. I think it could flare up again, although I hope it doesn't. I do think now we'd be more alert to the warning signs and would try to back off before things reached that point.

Annie too was very distressed by the resurrection of a pattern she'd hoped she'd left behind.

I have to acknowledge that there's something in me that is capable of going on and on relentlessly, driving things forward until they get out of control. It's like a self-destruct mechanism. I can be rational about it now, but when it sets itself in motion I think 'I don't care what happens, I'm just going to go on and on, and get angrier and angrier until I get the response I want.' Unfortunately there's something slightly similar in Jim, a tendency to latch on to some argument or standpoint and hang on to it grimly, allowing the other person no sway. I'm not convinced that he would acknowledge that about himself. If I'm feeling OK I just let the argument drop when he gets like that. But if I'm feeling vulnerable then it is dangerous. The only positive thing I can say about it is that we do recognise that pattern now, and its destructive potential.

It takes a lot of courage and self-awareness to admit your vulnerabilities in the way that Annie has had to do. And if recognising your weaknesses is hard enough, exposing them to another person is doubly difficult, because you run the risk of being laughed at, told not to exaggerate, belittled, or ignored. Even a trusted and loving partner can give the wrong reaction sometimes — he or she might not really understand what you are saying, may be preoccupied, or you might just choose the wrong moment. And because no one's likely to admit to their deficiencies unless they have to, you may well be asking for understanding and love at a moment when, because of your behaviour, your partner feels least like giving it. What's more, both of you may find it difficult to express love and affection at the best of times, especially if those feelings have led to disillusionment in the past.

James had been deeply hurt by his divorce, eight years before he met Jenny.

> When Jenny used to say that she loved me, I took it with a large pinch of salt. Often I wouldn't reply at all, and I hardly ever said that I loved her in return. I knew she needed my reassurance and commitment, but it was impossible for me to say it, even though it was what I felt. Somehow, the very fact of her saying she loved me touched a raw nerve that made me feel horribly knotted up inside.
>
> The whole idea of 'love' was an emotive one for me. When my marriage was on its last legs, my wife tried desperately to stop me leaving. There were endless scenes, and she kept saying that she loved me, as if that would make me stay. But what *I* meant by love and what she meant by it were two different things. Our marriage had broken down because we couldn't communicate with each other on any level — there was no understanding left between us to my mind. So to hear her talk of 'loving' me was risible and meaningless. Yet at the same time it was agonisingly painful, as the high hopes we'd had at the outset of the marriage had been completely dashed.
>
> Perhaps it was no wonder that I greeted Jenny's protestations of love with deep suspicion. I'd like to say that having faced up to all this, I was able to accept Jenny's love and communicate my own feelings to her. But that hasn't really happened. We do talk about it every so often and I think we feel surer now of each other's love, but I know we're both constrained when it comes to being more open about our feelings. I think it could take years to work out.

THE POWER OF THE PAST

Until James finally told Jenny about his experience with his wife, she'd been bewildered and distressed by his behaviour. Knowing the nature of the problem has helped, but she feels that there's still a long way to go.

He didn't exactly tell me — the whole thing suddenly erupted in a burst of emotion one night. We'd been having one of our regular, vague, wary conversations, which I was finding more and more exasperating. 'Look, I really do love you' I said, hoping for some positive response. Instead, he yelled 'You're just like that bloody woman!' I was confused and amazed and it took us the whole of a long sleepless night of talking before I finally got it all out of him. I think we were both shocked to have all his raw hurt, disappointment and rage out in the open.

It did help me to understand him better. Up until then he'd always seemed in control and it was almost as if he didn't care what either of us felt for the other. Then I realised that he actually cared very much. Before, I'd assumed he was unsure of his feelings towards me. That said, I still feel frustrated that we can't communicate openly as often as I would like. Still, it's early days yet, and I hope it will get easier — or perhaps less necessary — as we both gain confidence in our relationship's stability.

James is still mourning his dead marriage, a process which sometimes takes many years. Madeleine has also witnessed her partner's attempts to deal with his grief.

A great deal of mourning for the failure of his first marriage has had to be got through in my presence. He had been repressing this grief for so long that it was bound to come through in the end. Although it is painful to watch, as indeed to undergo, we both understand what is going on and regard it as necessary and healthy if regrowth is eventually to happen properly. I have dealt with this problem by being forbearing and loving when these inevitable griefs strike; talking them through without reservation and obtaining professional counselling.

Madeleine's belief in the possibility of regrowth is important. Life is a process of development and change. Many people, for instance, feel that they alter so much during their first marriage that by the time the relationship ends they have become 'a different person' from the one who got married in the first place. And there's no reason to suppose that similar growth doesn't continue in response to different circumstances that occur right through life.

Change, no matter how desirable, is daunting. Breaking old patterns involves probing the psyche — never a pleasant sensation. As all these people have discovered, recognising the problem is just the start, although it's probably the hardest part of all. Then comes the task of learning to live with the knowledge, of gradually exposing and examining painful feelings until you become less vulnerable to them, and they lose some of their power to hurt. It can't happen overnight. Knowing what makes you behave in a certain way doesn't mean the same thing won't happen again and again. But if you keep sight of why, then every time the situation arises and is controlled, you are building up strength for the future, and exorcising the ghosts of the past.

7. CHILDREN — LIVING REMINDERS

Problems for step-families and new families

One of the biggest areas of conflict in second marriages is the subject of children: those by a previous marriage; those that you have together; those that might have been, that the two of you are not able, or choose not, to bring into being. The fact that second marriages are at even greater risk of failure than first may well be connected with the fact that frequently at least one partner already has children, and this is bound to produce additional stresses and strains that aren't present for first-timers. The very existence of children, even if they live elsewhere, and their bond with their parent has to be accepted by a new partner, along with the implications of the financial, emotional and time commitments involved. And an existing family is an important factor when a new couple are considering whether or not to have children of their own.

FACING THE PROBLEMS

There's no easy, foolproof route to a happy relationship with children in tow. There are as many problems — and as many possible ways of tackling them — as there are couples, but two basic rules apply to everyone. First is the vital importance of discussing the whole area in detail *before* making a commitment: how often will you see them, and where; how much care are you expected to give; what are the financial implications; what happens at Christmas and holidays; where will the children stay; is there enough room; what sort of relationship are you hoping for between children and new partner; who has the right to administer discipline; will you have children of your own and if so, what about money, work, childcare? All these questions need to be brought out into the open and the search for answers at least begun. And that's only a beginning. Some questions just can't be answered, and the solutions to many others will only emerge in time.

Talking's all very well, but it's no substitute for experiencing the reality, and all your carefully made decisions may come to nothing in the face of the facts. You may well have agreed that smacking is out of order until your partner's four-year-old scribbled on your wallpaper. You were quite happy to keep a low profile when it came to teenage behaviour until your step-14-year-old fell through the door at 2 a.m. reeking of drink. You promised to put your partner first until your son phoned up and asked you to come to his school play on the same evening as your carefully planned dinner party. You thought you were ready to have a child but then your partner got cold feet. In the end, there's nothing to be done, except take a deep breath and deal with problems as they arise. The second rule is knowing while you do so that it's unsafe to take anything for granted, including your own future feelings. Talk, talk, talk, is the message, and not just at the beginning: 'Go over it again and again before you marry'; 'Make absolutely sure you know what you are letting yourself in for'; 'Don't underestimate the power of those children to come between you — be aware and try not to feel threatened'. Sentiments like these are constantly repeated.

It may sound glaringly obvious to suggest that couples might find it helpful to discuss their problems, but it's surprising how often people admit to retreating into resentful silence, expecting the other to mind-read; or taking the so-called 'easy' option of keeping quiet rather than 'rock the boat'. Yet most of these also confess that eventually anger and resentment fester until they erupt, often with disastrous effect, causing distress and damage to anyone within range. Better by far, most reckon, to say it when you think it, rather than let your partner go on in blissful ignorance of your innermost seethings.

Another helpful factor, seemingly often overlooked, is letting the children have a say, if they're old enough. Even young children have deep feelings about their parents' carryings on, and they have a right to give an opinion and to be included in discussion. 'Remember, they are more vulnerable than you are, and deserve to be treated with consideration. After all, they didn't ask to get dragged into all this,' says one step-parent. And another; 'Treat them with honesty and respect, don't foist your decisions on them, and you will have done all you can to oil the wheels of family life. But don't expect it to be easy.'

One thing to bear firmly in mind when weighing the pros and cons is that children frequently act as the catalysts that propel people into ill-advised relationships. Reasons *not* to embark on a new partnership include being fed up with coping with children on your own; wanting to provide children with a new 'parent'; panicking about impending age and lack of children. Yes, they are all reasons for seeking the right partner, but make quite sure that that is what you've found and not just someone who might do. 'Marry in haste, repent at leisure' is a maxim which should be on full view at every registry office. Even if it seems like a brilliant idea to rush into a marriage and solve all your problems with children at a stroke, you might just find that the alternative was preferable. One thing which has been proved over and over again the hard way is that children cannot hold together a shaky marriage, and nor should they be expected to.

If you're already in a second relationship and the children are causing you heartache, what can you do? Wait, is one answer: give it time and be patient. 'Children change as they grow up, and eventually they do leave the nest. The amount of time is finite, so try and bear with it until they fly,' said one exasperated stepfather. 'I'm prepared to keep working towards a better relationship with my partner's children, and I suspect it will get easier in time, especially as I become more secure with him,' said a slightly jaded stepmother.

If you've reached the stage where the children have driven such a wedge between the two of you that you can't reach each other any more, try to take a break together and thrash things out, away from the trouble. Or go to an outsider for help if the issue is too sensitive to approach direct. Simon:

> I reached my wits' end last year, and could not take any more of those kids and my wife's relationship with them. It was having a physical effect on me, and I was getting dreadfully tense and wound up. A friend recommended a masseur, who also helps you talk as you relax. Over a period of months it helped enormously. I'm much calmer about the whole thing now. It's by no means perfect, but it is bearable most of the time, which is a definite improvement.

It's all far easier said than done, and there are no simple solutions to the desperate tangles, misunderstandings and conflicts that people find themselves in over their children. However, it is sometimes possible to achieve harmony, even if territorial treaties have to be negotiated first.

Don't think twice before you embark on a new relationship where children are concerned: think 10 times. Try above all to consider the potential problems realistically. Children are around for a long time, and the demands they rightly make of their parents are not to be underestimated. Are you prepared to compromise, sacrifice and sometimes take second place? You may find the rewards are worth it, but ponder long and hard before you say yes.

CHILDREN — LIVING REMINDERS

HIS, HERS, OURS, THEIRS, MINE, YOURS

The permutations are numerous; there are couples who both have children by previous relationships, some or all of whom live with them; couples where one is a parent and the other is not; there are live-in children and those who visit, regularly or occasionally; children ranging in age from babes-in-arms to young adulthood and beyond; there are couples where one partner wants babies and the other doesn't; and there are children born into second marriages who call for yet more adjustments all round. Every situation is different, and each has its own potential hurts and disappointments, as well as potential for enrichment, growth and pleasure.

Children of past marriages are flesh-and-blood souvenirs and, unlike memories, they don't fade with time. This can be one of the hardest truths for a new partner to accept, especially if he or she is childless, and therefore a stranger to the world of parental bonds. There is little likelihood that a divorced parent can let the past gradually fade and slip away. Couples without children have a definite advantage here: although their previous marriages may well 'resurface' from time to time and cause some distress over the years, the pain has a chance to ease as the old life disappears into the realms of memory — once the divorce is over there's usually no further need for contact with ex-spouses, which in itself helps pave the way to a new future.

Where children are involved, however, there is scant opportunity to jettison the past totally. And it's not just the children who intrude on the new couple's togetherness. The ex-spouse can loom large as well. For a start, children who look or behave like an ex can be niggling, but potent, memory-joggers. Far worse is the regular contact involved in making practical arrangements. There's no forgetting an ex who's constantly on the phone, or turning up on the doorstep to collect the offspring. He or she can be a powerful source of disruption between the new partners.

In addition if the children are living elsewhere, then the

parent who is separated from them may well suffer guilt and remorse at having left them. However happy your present life with a new partner, there will inevitably be sharp and painful reminders of the lost family life to cope with. If the children visit, or are visited, seeing them may serve only to make the sense of loss more acute afterwards. And if you are childless, don't underestimate the pangs you will suffer if your new partner has bouts of depression or guilt over his or her children. Be aware, too, that your sympathy may well be tempered with, at best, irritation and incomprehension, at worst rabid jealousy. Primitive emotions are at work.

DUAL ROLES — PARENT AND LOVER

At the start of a relationship, new partners tend to see each other in the romantic role of lover. The existence of children can be an unpleasant intrusion into this starry-eyed interlude. Vicky had been separated for three years when she met Ian in London. There were no children from her marriage, but Ian had teenage children who lived with their mother in Cambridge.

> He used to go off on alternate Saturdays to see them, and I admit I didn't like it. At that stage our affair was in a very passionate, lovey-dovey phase, where we spent as much time together as possible, and I hated it when he disappeared for the whole day.
> To start with, though, the children didn't seem like real people to me. I hadn't met them and I preferred not to think about them too much. I saw them as a threat because I recognised that if it came to a conflict of interests, Ian would always put them before me. I couldn't accept that there was room for all of us in his life.
> I didn't meet any of the children for the first six months Ian and I were together. Although they came to London a couple of times, he preferred it if we didn't meet until we were fairly sure that our relationship was

stable. So when they were coming I had to clear my stuff out of his house and spend the night alone, feeling thoroughly fed up and at the same time, horribly guilty at the strength of my jealousy.

One small thing brought the fact of his parenthood home to me early on. I was making a coffee at his place, and one of the mugs had the word 'Dad' on it. Suddenly I realised that this man was someone's father, and I put the mug back, saying 'I don't think I'll use *that* one'. It wasn't just my envy of his love for them, but my feelings too, that it was somehow very unsexy for my man to be a dad. All very Oedipal I'm sure, and totally unreasonable — but very deep emotions which have been hard to overcome. At the time Ian said, 'If we stay together, you'll have to come to terms with it sooner or later'. He was right, but it has taken a conscious, hard effort on my part, and a growth in understanding and sensitivity on his, to make it happen.

If both partners have children, the acceptance of a dual role is usually easier, although there's still room for resentment. Tim and Harriet both have children from their first marriages. Tim:

> While my son visits every week, Harriet's 13-year-old daughter lives in — she's always there. We never seem to get any time on our own and, even if Rebecca's out, there's always worry over whether she'll get home all right, does she need to be picked up, and so on. I understand Harriet's concern, because I feel very protective towards Luke, my five-year-old. But we only have him for one day a week. Rebecca's a constant presence, and she doesn't go to bed until 10 at night! Harriet resents it too but at the same time she suffers guilt for finding her own daughter intrusive. It's one hell of a strain, and the three of us have terrible rows over it. So far we haven't worked out any solution.

Harriet tries hard to see things from her daughter's point of view.

To start with she was very sad about the divorce, but when she saw that my husband I were still friendly she settled down. She became closer to me — a bit clingy. She has been jealous of my new relationship with Tim which has been difficult, especially as she's also had to get used to her dad's girlfriend. She's starting to relax a bit now, and it looks hopeful. She's jealous too of Tim's little boy and he in turn has been a bit wary. It's a slow process for us all to get to know one another. We've decided to go away together in the summer — along with several bottles of tranquillisers — and I'm getting more confident that all will be well. At least I can talk to Rebecca to some extent about these problems because they affect her. Talking helps her to realise that she's still very important to me and hasn't been ousted by Tim.

Inevitably, as Tim and Harriet have found, divided loyalties tug fiercely at the heart, although this may ease as the children grow older and demand less undiluted attention. Alan's two boys occasionally stay with him and his wife. 'Problems include the lack of space, felt particularly by my wife. Occasionally I feel torn between them, although that seems less of a problem now.' And when Laura's younger son lived with her and Geoff: 'Sometimes relations between us were strained. Our house is small and we sometimes wished to do things which clashed. But we tried to talk through the problem and the relationship is now a very good one.'

THE POWER OF SPOUSES PAST

Sometimes when he comes back from visiting the kids he's furious because of something his ex-wife has said or done. Once, after he and I had been together for over a year, he suggested to her that two of the children come away to a friend's cottage with us. Her response was to say 'If you're going to be sharing a bed with that girl, then my children are not going to stay under the same

CHILDREN — LIVING REMINDERS

roof.' He was livid, I was hurt and angry — after all, we had a stable relationship, the kids knew me, and were hardly babies, but in their mid-teens. I was amazed at how strongly I felt her dislike of me, and her desire to wound both of us flooding towards me, even though we'd never met!

Ex-wives and husbands possess a powerful weapon, in the shape of the children, with which to manipulate the new marriage. Lucky are the couples who manage to sustain cordial relationships with their ex-spouses. Laura, for instance, doesn't mind if Geoff goes off to stay with his sons, who live with his ex-wife and her new husband and child. 'I don't object at all, as we have a very friendly relationship, and even exchange Christmas presents.' More common are situations where a mutual tolerance goes on, with no pretence at anything more. 'My wife displays a welcome frostiness when my ex-wife rings up', says one father.

For some, though, the ex-spouse can stir up endless strife. Harry is on bad terms with his ex-wife and they are battling out their maintenance agreement in court. His youngest son regularly visits Harry and his second wife, Rhoda, who finds the boy's questions disturbing:

Sometimes when he comes, he'll go round asking 'Is that new?', or 'What did that cost?' He's obviously primed by his mother beforehand. That doesn't make me feel too wonderful. He once asked me if I dyed my hair! And I have nothing but contempt for Harry's daughter. When the business of money flared up she rang and called me names over the phone. I said to Harry, 'you'll pay her over my dead body'. I'm not having a girl who's only met me once calling me names like that. They're only out of her mother's mouth, I know that, but they've been said.

Harry agrees: 'My daughter has totally disowned me and I never see her. She's like her mother, so I can understand why she's behaved like this.'

Children present a convenient, and usually innocent, vehicle for a bitter ex, who perhaps feels hard done by, to project his or her fury on to a second marriage. They can be used in many ways to twitch the leash, and remind a former husband or wife that the marital knot has not been severed completely. Judy:

> Last year, David's ex-wife engineered things so that one or other of the children was always away, right through the summer. There wasn't a single week when they would all be together to spend time with David, even though the access agreement stated that he should have them for *two* weeks every summer. The funny thing was that until then there'd never been a problem, throughout the 10 years they'd been apart. Then I came on the scene. Jill claimed she hadn't realised that the dates clashed, but David had asked her much earlier in the year to make sure that a week was left free and she still went ahead and made other arrangements.

New partners can find it disturbing if children chatter about the ex's doings. 'The less real their mother seems to me, the less threatening I find her,' said one new wife. And sooner or later, comparisons are bound to be made: 'We don't watch TV'; 'Mummy doesn't drink wine'; 'My daddy helps me with maths homework' — hurtful little barbs, which can easily find a vulnerable spot.

GUILT AND JEALOUSY

These unappealing emotions are frighteningly strong: hard to combat, harder still to keep in proportion, and not easily defused by rational argument. Guilt is usually the prerogative of the partner who has 'inflicted' the trauma of divorce on his or her children, although it can lurk too in the mind of a resentful new partner who can't get a grip on the antagonism he or she secretly feels towards the

CHILDREN — LIVING REMINDERS

children. Jealousy also belongs to the non-parental partner, over the love or material items which are lavished on the children. Such destructive feelings can wreak havoc in a relationship. Wendy had a daughter of her own, but her jealousy of Rick's daughter caused problems right from the start.

> I was always jealous of Rosemary; it was agony. He was so loving and sweet to her, and so cruel to my daughter, Felicity. He used to hit Felicity round the head; he'd say you should never hit a child and then he'd knock her about. She is very strong-willed and she can be a bit rude. She doesn't behave like a 'nice little girl'. I used to say, 'I wish you could treat them the same', and he'd say, 'But they're different children'.
>
> Rosemary is a goody goody. If someone kicks her in the shins she says, 'If I did that to you it would hurt a lot, so you should imagine what it's like for me.' She never hits anybody. By comparison, Felicity's a little thug, I suppose.
>
> I didn't confront Rick about it often. It was the only thing we could never discuss because he got angry. He insisted that we move to north London. I didn't want to go, but he wanted to be nearer Rosemary, who was living with her mother. I went to Marriage Guidance for about six months just to talk about my jealousy. It didn't really help me, and in a way it made Rick less precious to me. I didn't tell him that I was going, because I thought since he loved her so much, he would stop loving me if he realised just how jealous I was. I still hate Rosemary. I saw her recently and she doesn't look pretty. She used to, but now she's a bit gawky and has these funny screwed up eyes which her mother has. And I was pleased. That was terrible.

Hilary found out what it was like to be on the receiving end of her new partner's guilt and jealousy.

> My second husband was extremely jealous of my three

children, who lived with us, and, in the last two years we were together, did his utmost to alienate me from them. Although he blamed his ex-wife for the break-up of his marriage, he felt a lot of guilt about leaving his children. He was very unsure of their affection and tried to buy it with presents. They took advantage of this, as I suppose many children do, and then he began to resent them. At the same time, he tried to poison me against my children. We had a big fuss once when he read my daughter's diary, put it on tape and played it back to me. I thought this was a most despicable thing to do. My daughter never liked him or the way he treated me — maybe she was seeing 'echoes' of my first marriage. He showed his jealousy in that he resented my communicating with the children.

The marriage eventually broke up.

Some parents do seem able to leave their children behind when a marriage ends without feeling overwhelming guilt, or at least they are tough enough to suppress it. The only way for some to achieve this, however, is to sever links with the children. Harry:

We married because my wife was pregnant and it was wrong from the start, although we stuck it for 16 years. After I left I never felt any guilt or regret at all. I felt sorry for the children, but I realised they were better off without me. They weren't seeing anything other than arguments and unstable life. I've made a conscious decision that I have a new life to lead and that is my prime consideration. If they have to suffer, they will have to suffer. Maybe not financially, but there is a new life and that must go on because it's the future. If there has to be a choice, it must be the current marriage, not the children. It sounds hard, put in those terms, but I think you've got to decide that having left them with one parent, however much you'd like to see them, the first loyalty has got to be here. If it came to the point where Rhoda said, 'I never want you to see them again',

I'd have to think about that, but I would agree with it. I'd try to persuade her, but this new family must take priority. As it is, I don't see my two eldest, although I hope they will come round eventually. The youngest is willing to visit us, but it's very difficult to fit it in because I'm always having to work at weekends and it conflicts.

Harry may think that he's acting for the best in not seeing his children, but they may well feel differently. Laura's two sons certainly did when their father deliberately dropped contact with them after the divorce. Years later, now grown up, they are still distressed by his rejection of them, as Laura explains:

He has no communication with them, which they have never been able to understand. They view their father with disgust because he doesn't want to know them. He remarried within a year of our divorce and has a daughter by that marriage, who doesn't know that she has two half-brothers. He eventually moved away and his sons don't know his address or phone number. The eldest, in particular, has never understood why his father didn't want either of them.

LIVING TOGETHER

Couples who begin their new life together with the children under the same roof, may well find it harder to adjust and settle into life together than couples without children. 'There simply isn't the time or space for us,' said one new husband whose young stepson lives in. 'Jonathan always takes precedence. He's a nice enough kid, sure, but it was his mother I married, not him.'

There's nothing like living at close quarters to bring conflicts into play. The second partner who agrees to live *en famille* with the children of his or her spouse's first marriage is almost certainly taking on more than he or she bargained for. Romantic notions of ready-made family bliss can quickly crumble. The relationship between step-child and step-parent must be one of the most rewarding if it comes off, but one of the very hardest to achieve. Judith has

> two children who live with us. Although Clive has tried hard, they never really accepted him until their own father nearly died from a heart attack and Clive (being a doctor) was a great support. A lot of things were talked about then which previously had been swept under the carpet. Now they come to Clive much more for advice and I've stopped trying to act as middleman.

Combining two families is inevitably tricky. Diana and her two young daughters moved in with Malcolm and his two teenage sons with dire consequences.

> Problems arose with his children immediately we were married. One left home, the other will not speak to me. Malcolm does not support me in regard to his boys. I don't think my divorce has affected my children and people seem to find their behaviour normal for their ages. Mine are no problem, but Malcolm's want to have power over our lives. They are undisciplined, hateful and bitter and they would rather live with their mother, but she won't have them.

When Helen left her husband, who was having an affair with a much younger woman, she took with her their three daughters, aged nine, eight and six, and moved in with Richard, who was also divorced and whose youngest daughter, aged 12, was living with him at the time. 'It was appallingly difficult to adjust. We were packed into a small house, in a strange town, all trying to create a familiar and comfortable environment — impossible!' Thirteen years later, Helen looks back:

> We have had endless problems, compounded by the step-family difficulties. My children, although always

CHILDREN — LIVING REMINDERS

very close to me, resented their step-father as they went through the teenage phase. His eldest girl lived with us for 10 weeks but she was angry at her mother and her new partner — it was hell! The youngest girl, who is now at university, stays with us during vacations, as her mother has opted out, and that seems to be OK. One problem has been the impossibility of hiding my second husband's regular bouts of depression from my children. I have had also to try to get them to tolerate his partiality for his own children and lack of affection for them — this is easier now they are older.

With a bit of luck, problems diminish as children grow older, but for many families the step-relationship is never a happy one, and they just have to accept that there will be a rocky ride for a few years. It seems certain that successful step-families seldom emerge quickly, and can take years to find an acceptable mode of living. Lesley and Andrew were married five years ago, and Lesley's two young sons from her first marriage live with them. 'At the beginning, the kids did their utmost to come between us, in all sorts of subtle, and not-so-subtle, ways. I know Andrew found it very hard to settle down with them. Things are better now, but it has been harder than either of us imagined.' Andrew agrees:

> If I'd known what it was going to be like . . . I was totally naive, and had no real idea of what to expect from living with Lesley's kids. They were so manipulative and at times I could have cheerfully strangled them. Fortunately Lesley was very supportive, and did her best to keep the peace. In time, we settled down together, fairly peacefully, but it has taken years. We've found a level of co-existence that seems to work, but although I'm much fonder of the boys now, I'll never love them as if they were my own.

When children are tiny, you do at least stand a chance of influencing them and gaining their acceptance. Young children are extraordinarily adaptable, and this can make things easier. Teenagers are a different kettle of fish. New partners who move in on a family of adolescents had better beware: these young people have strong opinions and are often well-practised at the art of game-playing; they may be loveable, funny and stimulating — challenging, even — but also alarmingly hard to control or understand, often the more so when they are not your own. 'They're like aliens from another planet,' said one mid-thirties stepmother of her newly acquired teenagers.

They possess enormous confidence, and they're awfully leggy and fashionably dressed. They stride in, usually accompanied by great gangs of friends, go through the fridge like locusts, and disappear upstairs to play loud and discordant music. I feel like an old fogey, and I find them rather intimidating, they're surrounded by such a powerful aura of adolescence. And yet they can also be endearingly childlike and immature — it's exhausting to live with!

One difficulty with teenagers can be finding a suitable role for the step-parent to play. To try to become a substitute, or additional 'mummy' or 'daddy' is generally inappropriate, and to compound the difficulty, your partner may be equally at sea as to where you stand in the family. Says Simon, of his partner's 13- and 14-year-old:

There's no way you can befriend hostile teenagers. I become superfluous whenever the children are around, because I have no role to play, and my partner goes on to auto-parent whenever they're there. I like the kids well enough as individuals, but I can't work out how to relate to them. I think I was very green at the beginning. I thought I'd be able to love them, and that they'd love me, and we'd have this wonderful relationship, with none of the pressures of parenthood. What a joke! Yet my partner can't really understand what I'm on about. She doesn't seem to realise that she turns into someone else — a mother — when the kids are there, and that by doing so she excludes me. It's all very difficult and painful. To be honest, I can't wait until the kids leave home.

VISITING TIMES

When the children are not resident with the new couple, but visit, or are visited, any problems become disjointed, and may disappear between times, only to revive when the next meeting comes round. However, there may be positive advantages for the new partner in having regular contact with the children. Madeleine lives with David. His son, aged seven, and three-year-old daughter visit them regularly.

> There are no apparent signs of damage from their parents' divorce, and both children seem to have taken very warmly to me, although I am sure that the questions and difficulties will come — about why Daddy and Mummy could not get on, and why Daddy loves me instead. I see them every weekend (they stay alternate weekends). The seven-year-old was a bit cheeky ('trying it on') at first, but that stopped when he found he liked me, and when his granny (who likes me very much) showed that she regarded me as her son's partner and a family member.

For others, the saving grace is the fact that the children are *not* permanent residents. Maggie acquired five step-children, now grown-up, all of whom lived with their mother.

> I see them at least twice a year. The eldest daughter is still unsettled by the divorce. She sees herself as the linchpin of the whole family and jealously guards the family integrity. She always has one hysterical outburst per visit. I am trying to improve my relationship with her. I'm on better terms with the others, especially since

their mother remarried. But as a family they tend not to talk about their feelings, which I find difficult.

Sometimes even liking the children would be a bonus. Rhoda:

I've met Harry's children once, but we didn't get on. They played a game that I was invisible. I never saw the two eldest again. It was pretty disastrous because they'd made up their minds. It was a really dreadful day; they wouldn't give it a chance. I couldn't have coped if they'd lived with us. The younger boy visits, but there have been problems and I have resented him at times.

Russell's girlfriend, Liz, finds her stepson's visits intolerable, and a threat to the whole relationship.

When Russell and I moved into a studio flat together, his ex-wife suddenly said that their son could spend every weekend with us. We were told by her solicitor that her intention was to put pressure on our relationship and split us up. My stepson was openly hostile at first. He demanded attention almost constantly, and if ever James showed me any signs of affection he would pull us apart. He told me I was not allowed to touch him or kiss him or play with his toys. It is now over two years since Adam started to spend weekends with us and our relationship has only improved fractionally, if at all. He is not so overtly nasty to me now, but I believe that is because he is confident of his position. I was not at all prepared for the real hostility and unpleasantness which I encountered. I did not know how to handle his unkind remarks and chose to ignore them. I was too shocked and inexperienced to confront him and ask him why he said such things. I did not discuss any of the problems I was experiencing with Russell, who was delighted with the way we all appeared to be getting along. When I did admit to him what was happening he said he would reprimand Adam. But Adam denied everything and Russell accepted his explanation. My worst fears were confirmed — Russell was incapable of standing up to his own son and of taking my side against him. Adam is the only problem I don't feel able to handle. Without him I am sure we would have had a successful relationship.

Less of a strain than regular stop-overs, but still a problem in their own way, are situations where the absent parent (usually the man), leaves his new partner behind while he visits his children at the former marital (or another) home. Vicky explains:

Ian visits his children every other week, and he's away all day. Do I mind? Yes and no. Sometimes, if it's been a busy week, I'm happy to have some time on my own to unwind and relax quietly. Other times I'd like to be with him and feel lonely while he's away. Either way, it always gives me a pang when he walks out of the door. It's silly, but even if I've had a good day on my own, or with friends, it's still difficult to readjust when he gets home. I think it's right that he should see the children, but I do resent it sometimes, because weekends are so precious. Of course, it's deeper than that really. I'm not just fed up because he's been away, but because I feel his relationship with his children to be a threat to us, although I can't easily explain how. At the same time, it raises all sorts of questions in my mind about the future — suppose one or other of his kids made big demands on us — wanted to move in for a while, say. Could I cope? There's always a lot going on under the surface where the children are concerned.

The distress felt by a parent on leaving the children can also rub off on the partner who stays behind.

Usually when he comes back he's a bit low and distant, because he's left them — he's grieving for them in a way. He rarely admits to just how much he misses them, and how much he knows he loses out when he's not with them. Not surprisingly, we can't comfort each other properly, because so much of it is too difficult to acknowledge. So the whole business often causes an unspoken rift that can take a day or two to heal.

Helen finds Richard is affected similarly when he has visited his three daughters. 'He was granted fortnightly access, for Saturday or Sunday. He is always emotionally exhausted afterwards. Fortunately for me, my own children live with us, and this helps me to cope with his depression.'

Sometimes it's the children who disappear to visit their absent parent. 'It always takes a day or so to regain our closeness when they come back from visiting their father,' says one mother; and 'My daughter is very hard to handle after being with my ex-husband,' says another. 'He spoils her emotionally and physically, and she comes back behaving in a very high-handed way, and looking fat!'

THE HORROR OF HOLIDAYS

Christmas and holidays, far from being the happy, harmonious times portrayed in popular mythology, have a knack of bringing to a head differences that exist all year round and roar up to the surface in the heat of all the surrounding excitement. Annual excursions and festivities can throw together families who otherwise spend the year apart, to shattering effect. 'The first Christmas we were all together,' remembers Simon, 'my wife's kids excelled themselves when it came to playing one of us off against the other. By the end of the break we were both at the end of our tethers, and we took ourselves off on a week's holiday together, just to recover.'

If the children live elsewhere, the annual question of where they will go for Christmas can be explosive. Sarah says:

One solution was for Sean to do a crack-papering exercise, and spend the day with his ex-wife and kids, just like they did in the old days. Which was all very well, but it left me high and dry, and forced me to resort to the long and ignominious trail home to mother. It was miserable. But it seems there's no way we can ever do what I would like, which is to spend Christmas quietly together, at home. Every year, around October, I start to get nervous, knowing that the annual negotiations are going to start at any minute, bracing myself not to feel rejected. I'd like to put a permanent ban on Christmas.

Holidays can have the same sort of divisive effect. To go together; to take the kids; to go separately? Whichever you opt for, someone's going to feel hard done by. Helen's three children went on holiday with her and Richard for several years at the beginning of their marriage. 'They came with us until they were 16, but it wasn't very satisfactory and, if anything, intensified the split in the family.'

Certainly, if a relationship is already feeling a strain, a combined holiday is not a good idea, as Sue and Tom discovered. Sue:

With hindsight I can see what a bad idea it was. We had a lot of unresolved problems about our own future and the pressure of attempting to live as a family with teenagers who I hardly knew, was too much. It was fine for Tom, he could just get on with being a parent. But I didn't fit in anywhere. He was inhibited with me when they were there; I was bored by the sorts of things they wanted to do and felt totally out of it. The kids didn't like it if Tom and I went off on our own, and, worst of all, Tom actually didn't want to go off with me. I think I'd expected it would be like the two of us on holiday together, with the kids somewhere in the background. But what I got was that family, with me on the sidelines, looking on. I was in such an emotional state the whole time that I didn't know where to start to make things better. I was full of guilt and inadequacy, mingled with furious resentment and hurt. It was the loneliest two weeks of my life. We split up for a while afterwards — neither could see the other's point of view, and we were both very angry with each other. After we got back together we sorted out some other difficulties, which helped to cement our relationship. The issue of the children is still a sensitive one. I hope I'll be able to build up a relationship with them as individuals, gradually.

Plenty of step-families do enjoy their holidays together, however. 'Fine, except for one fracas'; 'The seven-year-old loves coming with us because we plan a mixture of entertainment and education on trips; his mind gets exercise in ways he enjoys and doesn't get at home, and this is a plus for all of us.' Every family is different.

STEPPING BACK

Sometimes the most workable solution is to keep children and second partner separate, perhaps with occasional brief meetings. If cash allows a compromise, then one partner can holiday with the children while the other goes away with friends or alone. The two can then take a break together at a different time of year. Expensive, yes — but less explosive. 'In the end, I decided that I just couldn't take too much exposure to the children. The odd day now and then is just about manageable, but in the main it's better if I keep out of it and let them have their mother to themselves,' said Simon. 'I don't see that changing until they become adults.' Still, it is a bit sad if there has to be such a gulf. How pleasant it would be if any step-family, however loosely defined, could blend itself together into a happy, homogenous whole. Unfortunately, there's no rule that says step-children have to adore their step-parents and vice versa. If they achieve a cordial and tolerant co-existence, meeting from time to time, but not attempting to emulate a parental bond, then that may be as much as it's realistic to hope for — and it is, after all, a great deal.

No one should blame non-parental partners who can cope with the daunting business of step-children only by standing back a bit, especially in the early years, so long as they don't attempt to come between parent and children. It takes a lot of time, a lot of exposure to each other, a lot of effort, to make a relationship between step-child and step-parent. Bridges can't be built overnight and have to be tackled slowly, at a speed which suits the individuals concerned.

THE PRICE OF LOVE

Money is the root of much bitterness. Hefty maintenance payments can really clobber a family's income, as can the financial burden of caring for an extended brood of step-children. When Helen and Richard married, they had between them six children, three of whom lived at home full-time. 'Money has been scarce until very recently as the children have grown up and left. Things are only better now that I am free to work,' says Helen. 'Financial worries took their toll on our relationship, and caused various problems, including sexual difficulties.' Harry's money problems stem from continued disagreements about his obligations to his ex-wife and family.

> She is now remarried and we are going through the courts about the maintenance. We had a bitter fight. She cried because she was worried about her financial security. It wasn't me she wanted, it was my money and worldly possessions. At the moment we are fighting over maintenance for my daughter. We settled on £27 a week for each of the three children. I still pay for the two boys, but stopped paying for my daughter when she started getting the full grant. Rhoda would lynch me if I carried on paying and also I don't see why my daughter should get the grant and maintenance as well. It's just money, money, money.

Rhoda resents the hold that Harry's ex-wife retains: 'The money Harry shells out on her and the children is our biggest problem. I find it difficult even now accepting that Harry pays so much to support his ex-wife and her new husband in their lovely big four-bedroomed house. The house they live in and the house we live in are two worlds apart.' Harry:

> Yes, I was living in a well-equipped home. Yet they still can't afford anything. I think that's what we find too upsetting. They're very consumer-orientated, their house has got five televisions in it, a couple of videos, five hi-fis. All the children have a complete set; the boys have TV in their bedrooms. It's ludicrous that they even consider they have a problem with money. You do get to the stage where you resent them, and you wonder if they are having the money for the right reasons. I don't think we'd object if the children were getting all the money and were totally taken care of. But we know very well now that it is going to support my ex-wife's new marriage which already has two incomes, and that shouldn't be necessary. I don't pay maintenance to her for herself, but it's the inflexibility of the courts to recognise that needs change greatly. They only seem to recognise that needs change in one way and that is in favour of the ex-wife. Or up, from my point of view. My solicitor has told me that it is almost impossible to get a maintenance order reviewed down, but I'm fighting that on what I consider to be very moral ground.

Despite the maintenance Harry pays, he can afford to support Rhoda and their own young son. For others, money difficulties make the difference between being able to start a family, and not being able to afford the loss of an income. This is the case for Marian, whose husband is supporting his non-working ex-wife and twin girls. She tries to be philosophical about it: 'One must be realistic about not having everything. I now have so much in comparison with the bleakness of previous years, I am happy to compromise in this area, even though I do feel a natural disappointment that it is unlikely I shall have a child by the man whom I dearly love. One can't help one's hormones.'

CHILDREN OF YOUR OWN

Couples who have no children of previous marriages are in for an easier time of it, if they decide to produce a family of their own. But even for them, the past can still have its influence. Sally didn't feel any desire for motherhood during her first marriage:

> But that was probably because there were so many problems that it was out of the question. I knew deep down that eventually I would have to get out. My problem sounds silly, but because my first husband was consistently unfaithful, right through the marriage, I find it very difficult now to trust my second husband. I've no reason to suspect that he would play around. I thought when I had a baby it would make him love me even more, and it hasn't. He still loves me, yes, and he's devoted to our daughter, but it hasn't stopped me feeling uneasy when he goes out in the evening. It hasn't set the seal of security on our relationship that I'd hoped for.

If the new baby joins a family of step-brothers and sisters, there may be the predictable problems of rivalry and favouritism. But the advent of parenthood can help the step-parent to appreciate what his or her partner feels about the other children. Bridget found that her two step-sons quickly took to Angie, the new baby, and her own attitude changed. 'I was jealous of the boys before I had my own child because they got so much attention from their father. Having Angie means that someone depends on me. I'm not jealous any more, and I understand my husband's relationship with his sons far better.' Judith found that the daughter of her second marriage, 'is the best thing that has ever happened to any of us — Clive, me and my two other children. She is very much loved by everyone and in turn loves us all.' However, for Jenny, who has a daughter from her first marriage, having children with her second husband has given rise to difficulties: 'At first my husband treated his step-daughter well. However, when he produced two daughters of his own the relationships within the family became fraught. The problems were blamed on the situation... I would say, "You don't love her as much as the others because she's not your child". I would be very rich if I had £1 for every time I have uttered those words.'

Couples who already have several children between them may decide not to have any more, however much they'd like to. This is perhaps an easier decision to reach if both partners already have children. Helen: 'I wanted us to have a child but Richard said we had enough already! (We each had three.) With hindsight I can see he was right (and he doesn't really care for children very much!).'

It can be desperately hard to reach an acceptable compromise if one partner already has children, and is reluctant to have more. Many's the second wife who has sacrificed her desire for motherhood, whether for financial or other reasons. This soul-searching decision can put a deep strain on the relationship. Alan, who has two sons:

> One difficulty early on in my second marriage was deciding whether to have a child. My wife wanted to, as she has no children, but also wanted my enthusiastic commitment. In the end it proved medically so improbable that we decided against the hassle involved. But we had counselling to help us over that one. I definitely feel that you should talk this over thoroughly before you decide to marry.

While Madeleine has no children from her first marriage, her partner has two from his.

> I don't think I will feel it fair either on him or them to

disrupt our growing sense of family happiness with his children when they visit, by having a child of our own. Also, I'm 38 now, having been a busy professional all my working life. I simply don't have much longer left for having a baby after first allowing my partner his emotional recovery time, much needed to get over the traumas induced by a bad first marriage, which have inevitably affected his relations with his children. Provided my relationship with him remains sound, and provided I can sustain happy step-relations with his children, this must suffice (and will, since I'm essentially a conjugal rather than a parental type, however good I may be with children).

Sue was hoping that life would make the decision for her.

I've always felt ambivalent about children. In my fantasies I used to end up with a man of roughly my own age, who had no children, or just one or two, and who wanted a family. That would have forced the issue, although I'm not sure how happy the outcome would have been. Instead I'm living with a man who's 14 years older than I am, already has a sizeable family who are in their teens. Although he doesn't rule out completely the idea of having more, I know he doesn't really want any, and I don't blame him — he's done it all, and who wants to start the nappy routine again when they're pushing 50? It is still a difficult issue for me, and will be, on and off, I suppose, until the menopause strikes.

Tom sympathises with Sue's dilemma. 'I think in many ways she'd welcome children, although I accept her view that she should only have them if she's wholehearted about the idea. It's not something you can sort out once and for all — feelings change, so we'll just have to wait and see.'

Often people make decisions about parenthood during

their first marriage which have to be changed, or at least questioned, during their second. Harry had three children by his first marriage, but his second wife, Rhoda, had none in hers. He wasn't too keen on starting another family to begin with, 'especially as we'd thought we wouldn't be having children because I'd had a vasectomy while I was married.' Rhoda: 'I'd accepted that there wouldn't be any babies when we married, but I changed my mind. I don't know why, it's just something to do with being a woman. And also, I know it's cruel to say it, but because Harry is 14 years older than me I was very worried about being left on my own.' Harry:

> So I had the vasectomy reversed and fortunately the operation worked and Rhoda was pregnant within six months. I had a lot of misgivings, having had one family. At my age, it's pleasant not to have any ties. I know all the pitfalls, and you're going to be tied for 10 years. We decided we'd only have one, although Rhoda did put some pressure on a few months ago for another. But I only wanted one — two are more demanding, and it's a lot easier to get rid of one, you're not so restricted as you are with a larger family. And I know what happens when I give in to something I don't really want to do — it can have dramatic implications. I really enjoy Matthew now that he's old enough to enjoy. I think we've resolved our needs quite nicely.

Rhoda: 'I agree with that. I would have liked another, but I wouldn't like Harry to have any more children after he's 40.'

THE PLUS POINTS

Despite all the tears and traumas, upsets and misunderstandings, many people find that in one way or another, children are an unexpected bonus in their second relationship and a source of great pleasure. Laura, whose two grown-up boys visit frequently:

CHILDREN — LIVING REMINDERS

It was more difficult at first, but now the boys are older they've accepted Geoff and have a very good relationship with him, especially my younger son. Both he and Geoff love music, and they play the piano and sing together and have tremendous fun. My one regret about my relationship with Geoff is that we are too old to have children together.

Andrew, who lives with Rachel and her two boys: 'It is possible to create a secure and happy family, and there's a great satisfaction in overcoming the hurdles to achieve that.' Charlotte didn't contemplate motherhood in her unhappy first marriage. Second time around was different, and she's delighted with her new role. 'I never realised how much I would love Katy. I've no regrets about having her.'

8.
HAPPILY EVER AFTER?

What *is* the secret of making it work? Do the people who achieve a successful second relationship have anything in common? The answer is that they have not allowed the failure of their first marriage to destroy them. They may feel regret and an abiding sense of sorrow, yes, because those are part of the legacy of a divorce. At the same time, though, they have seized the opportunity to learn from the experience, no matter how painful that process is. Having faced the failure and the reasons for it, they've discovered that it *is* possible to go forward better equipped to deal with the conflicts of life as half of a couple, and also readier to appreciate the pleasures.

We are all broken reeds, all damaged in some way by our pasts, but that doesn't mean that we can never relate happily with others again. Instead, we can be brave enough to examine what went wrong, and target our expectations more realistically in future. We can use time spent alone to build a strong sense of self-reliance and to come to terms with our fears of solitude and loneliness. Once in a new relationship we can consciously practise compromise and communication, skills which may have been lacking before. We can begin to understand the real meaning of a commitment — what it demands of us and the rewards it brings. We can put the past away, without having to bury it so deep that it is never mentioned again. We can allow it to influence the present positively, and we can even use the new relationship to work out old unresolved problems, in a different, safer, setting.

Understanding and acceptance of ourselves and our partners, a firm foundation of love, a real commitment —

these are the ingredients that give a second relationship a chance to outwit the statistics. They are none of them easy. The day will never arrive when we can say: 'This is exactly the way the relationship should be, and from now on it will be like this all the time.' Success is much more elusive and fragmented, and alternates with reversals, old patterns, fights and misunderstandings. We may get it right one day and get it wrong again the next day and the day after. Or we might have a 'good phase' lasting weeks or months, followed by a colossal storm.

It's a cliché to say that relationships have to be worked at, but it's true. For there's no such thing as a problem-free relationship. From practical differences over cash or washing up, through step-family wrangles, to assorted emotional eruptions which are hard to explain and harder still to deal with constructively: second relationships have to contend with the lot. The good news is that many people overcome the odds. Couples can and do succeed together where both have failed before.

THE SECRETS OF SUCCESS

Of those who rate their second relationship as unqualified successes so far, all have had to tackle a variety of problems and some have had a long struggle to reach a state of equilibrium. There are many conclusions, learned from the experience of divorce and re-coupling.

For example, Rachel, married for five years to a man with one divorce behind him, was finding it increasingly difficult to communicate. There were many upsets over his son, and she also had to adapt to life in a foreign environment with little support from her husband. After the divorce she spent five years alone and is now happily married to a man eight years younger than she is, who has not been married before. They have young twins.

I've had to acknowledge that the past is part of me, and I have had to deal with it. It's important to accept the past and learn from it, to talk about it and examine it, not try to leave it behind. In the time after my divorce I devoted a lot of energy to things which meant a lot to me, like work, politics and music, and developed those things. That gave me a solid foundation of self-worth from which I could safely examine the past and begin to understand it. It was useful preparation for the future as well.

I learned a lot from the whole experience. The problems I have with Mike aren't similar to those I had with Sam, because this time they are based on real things. I have very high expectations of the relationship and Mike knows that. It's tough on him, but it's also a sign of respect for him. We deal with things by talking about them honestly, however difficult that might be.

Veronica has been with her second partner for 13 years. She married first at 21 despite her misgivings, and stayed in that unrewarding relationship for 19 years.

A marriage should be between two adults who can listen, disagree, discuss and still remain good friends. Sex is an important part of the relationship and is something to be enjoyed by both partners, not demanded by men only. It was really wrong to marry my first husband. I knew all about him before we married and that he wouldn't be likely to change.

Tom and his first wife were so much at loggerheads that the relationship eventually broke down completely and he left. His second partner, Sue, has been divorced for six years. She and Tom have been together for three years and weathered many storms in their volatile relationship. Tom says:

It hasn't always been easy, but I realise now that I have to understand my partner and accept her, and she has to understand and accept me and my past. It's sometimes hard to remember that I am relating to another adult person, with very definite views of her own, and not a housewife or mother who is content to let me make the decisions.

Sue had overwhelming problems trying to communicate with her first husband.

I try harder with this relationship, although I don't always get it right. I've grown up a lot since my divorce, I'm not so rigid, so determined always to get my own way. I've made a real commitment to this relationship and I'm prepared to put a lot of effort into it, and to try and solve the problems constructively, as they arise. Tom feels the same way, and it is very rewarding to see the evidence that both of you are really trying hard. There are differences sometimes, and I'm sure there always will be, but we certainly have fewer rows now and are both more prepared to compromise.

Charlotte is married to Nick, who has not been married before. They have a young baby. She feels that she has been permanently scarred by her five-year marriage to a man with whom she had been deeply in love despite the fact that he was violent, unfaithful, and an alcoholic.

I've changed, I'm less tolerant and more confident. Before, I was frightened of being on my own and now I know I can cope. In a way that helps this relationship, because I'm not so clingy and desperate. The first marriage was very passionate, but not so mature. I hope this one is more equal. I feel sorry for Nick sometimes, because I don't think I'm always as understanding to him as I should be. I used to try and compromise more in my first marriage just to keep the peace. Now I'm not sure that I always try and work things out from Nick's point of view. I suppose if we have a problem or get on each other's nerves we try and sort it out together, and that helps.

Marrying again has been the best thing I've ever done and I'm very happy. I wanted to live with Nick because

I didn't want the hassle of getting out of it if anything went wrong. But he wanted to get married. There is something quite definite about taking that step. If you live together you still have some freedom which could make the relationship more exciting. Marrying was a big step for me but I'm very glad I did because I think it made Nick's attitude to me different and better. He thought now we can get on and build something. I don't think we'd have had children or bought a house if we weren't married.

Judith was first married at 24. Her husband, who had three children, was consistently unfaithful. They married because she was pregnant, although she also had romantic illusions about the nature of marriage. Her second husband has not been married before. They have one child.

I'm just a bit tougher now, but I still look at marriage through rose-tinted glasses. Maybe I've grown up as a result of my experiences. This time I was looking for a partner who had the same feelings about life, and I'm very happy, yes. It is definitely a success. We talk for hours about the children and also about my other problem, which is a constant need to prove my worth.

Joanne didn't marry for the first time until she was 27, but the marriage was a traumatic disaster. She extricated herself fairly rapidly from the clutches of a husband who maltreated her and behaved violently and completely unpredictably. Friends were uncertain about her second choice, Charlie, a divorced man with one son, and there have been problems over money and his attitude to work. However, they have stayed together and she rates the relationship a success.

I am deeply suspicious of all people now, and therefore cautious. It's madness to rush into things. You should get to see the person in all possible situations and predicaments before you decide. I first met Charlie nearly 20 years ago, after his first marriage broke up, although we were only acquaintances. In all, we knew each other for 13 years before we got married and we lived together for the last six of those. I felt I knew him pretty well, warts and all, and that I could manage him. There haven't been any nasty surprises since we got married and the difficulties we have had over money were very predictable.

Geoff left his first wife 16 years ago when he discovered her attachment to another man. Geoff moved out, leaving behind his twin sons, and his wife subsequently remarried. Geoff's second partner, Laura, has also been divorced. Her first husband was occasionally violent, and the couple were never able to communicate well. After the separation he deliberately severed links with their two sons. Laura lived on her own with the boys for 10 years, and enjoyed her independence. She and Geoff have been together for six years. Geoff:

We knew each other for about 15 months before I moved in. She was refreshingly frank in everything we discussed and her enthusiasm was infectious — she took 20 years off my age. I couldn't think of anyone else I'd want to live with, and that seemed a good starting point. The chief lesson I've learned is not to be afraid of broaching any matter which could give rise to a difference of opinion. I hope I never take Laura for granted.

Laura:

I can honestly say that there have been no serious difficulties. My main fear was that I would lose my independence, and at first I did crave time on my own. Gradually, though, Geoff has built up his own interests and now he often goes out without me so I get the house to myself for a few hours. It's important to have common interests but also to do things separately and not live in each other's pockets. I think I grew up towards the end of my first marriage and while I was on my own, I became much more assertive.

The end of Maggie's first marriage came as a devastating blow to her. There had been problems throughout the 10 years it lasted, but she still loved her husband and found it almost impossible to accept his complete rejection of her and their life together when he left her for another woman. She spent eight years picking up the pieces before marrying a divorced man with five children. There have been problems over money, sex and the children, but now, aged 58, she is happy and contented.

I've hung on to my separate, adult identity and not been tempted to live someone's else life. I've learned something from my divorce, definitely. For instance, my second husband doesn't use emotional blackmail on me as my first did, but if he did I would be able to stop him. Also, I was persuaded to keep everything secret when my first marriage was threatened. I would not do any such thing again. I feel more confident now, and braver, less afraid to bring things out into the open.

Boredom brought about the end of Eleanor's first marriage of 10 years. The catalyst was an affair, and she subsequently married the man for whom she left her husband. 'I have learned to be less selfish and more tolerant. I have grown up. Our arguments have centred mainly around my daughter — my tendency to give in to her versus my partner's idea of discipline. We've talked about it a lot and gained in understanding of each other.'

Alan's first marriage lasted 11 discontented years until his wife met someone else. On the rebound, Alan briefly and disastrously married a woman from a different culture. That marriage soon ended, and he didn't start to feel back on an even keel for another four years, when he met his third wife.

I had no reservations about this marriage, because she accepted me for what I am. And we were together for four years before we married. I realise now that you have to look for the right person for the real you, not the you you'd like to be . . . but then you have to know yourself. And I hope I've learned to be less selfish — that follows on I suppose from knowing myself better. Our biggest problem has been over whether or not to have a child, and we needed counselling to help us over that one. We've coped well with other potential problems like money, sex, independence, arguments and housework.

Madeleine's first marriage of 15 years died because of her husband's 'lack of interest' and insoluble sexual problems. Her present partner, also divorced, has two children. They have not yet married, but plan to do so.

I regret that my first marriage happened, in a sense, although it has been a very educational process for me. I wish I'd been more decisive about getting out years earlier. I realise now that the sexual aspect of marriage is vital. It shouldn't be the basis of the relationship but it is a very important bonding factor when all the other qualities are right. There is bound to be pain and sadness at previous failure and there will, because there are children, be continuing practical and emotional minefields to be tiptoed over. But having found someone as good and loveable as my Jack I feel I've got a head start!

Stories like these are heartening, not least because they present success as something achievable, constituting a mixture of triumphs and defeats. None of them is a picture of unalloyed joy, of happy couples strolling hand in hand into the sunset. Each one is a story of ground given, boundaries agreed, problems overcome, but not without a struggle, an ongoing relationship that is still changing and developing, still delivering new challenges to keep the partners on their toes. There are obviously strong bonds of love and affection there, but between the lines are tales of prolonged negotiations to reach the stage where these people can say, 'So far it's a success, and we're hopeful for the future'. What comes across is the importance of sheer hard work, far above the romantic elements of hearts and flowers.

A QUALIFIED SUCCESS

Some people say of their second relationships: 'I suppose it's a success, but . . .' It isn't a downright disaster, or at least not yet, but problems are looming which are potentially threatening. Lisa is still on friendly terms with her husband from whom she's been separated for three years. Their marriage broke up because of sexual problems and they share custody of their daughter. Lisa was on her own for a couple of years before meeting Richard, also divorced and with one son, at a party. After only six months he gave up his flat and moved into her house.

> The main problems are that I earn more than he does, and friction over his son and my daughter. Adjustments are difficult, but I hope we can deal with these difficulties by talking about them. Emotionally and physically I'd say, yes, my hopes and expectations have been fulfilled, but I suspect that other areas of dissatisfaction will arise. Nevertheless, I think and hope that it will be a success.

There's more than a hint of trouble here, which needs confronting soon, before too much resentment takes root.

Helen's 13-year first marriage ended when her husband fell for a much younger girl. Helen moved in with her second partner Bill almost immediately, after knowing him for only three months. Both had children, both were still distressed by their marriage break-ups. It's been tough, although the marriage has survived 15 years. Helen is philosophical.

I was blissfully happy when the children were young and I am most nostalgic for that phase of my past. Bill's first marriage was less satisfactory and I would say he is happier and more fulfilled with me. Not surprisingly I was quite emotionally upset for some time after my marriage broke up, and Bill has suffered from depression to a greater or lesser extent all the time we have been together. I realise now how immature and unrealistic I was at the start of our relationship. I have different expectations and priorities now and I try to change and adapt myself, rather than him. My reaction to problems and distress has been to intensify my religious commitment and expect more of God and less of husbands!

Lynn has had a lot of step-family problems in her second marriage. She says the relationship is successful, but:

It is not easy when there are two families of children mixed. I had reservations about it from the start — would it work, would the children get on; financial complications. I've learned not to be so independent, to show my feelings more and ask for more help. We have dealt with our problems by talking and arguing, but it is very hard when it comes to the children, who should believe who.

Gill had sex problems in her first marriage: her husband blamed her for being frigid and refused to take any responsibility for their difficulties. Her relationship with her second husband has been troubled by numerous problems and disagreements and, although over the years they have done a lot of sorting out, some resentments still rankle. However, Gill is prepared to accept the relationship for what it is, faults and all. 'I was playing at life before. This is real, for all its ups and downs. I was looking for security, someone to take care of me, fun, love and humour. Some hopes and expectations have been fulfilled and we are happy mostly, with reservations. It's not a brilliant success for me, although he insists he's very happy.'

Can these people improve their relationships? Perhaps not, where a fundamental difference of attitude is concerned, as for Lisa and her non-earning partner, or Helen and her depressed husband. The outcome will depend on the individuals; while some people seem resigned to staying put in a relationship that is at best only reasonably satisfactory, others feel a strong hint of growing unease and these relationships may well not last the course.

SECOND-TIME FAILURES

There are second-time disasters, mis-matches, bad decisions — the failures. Often, as with failed first marriages, the problems are obvious right from the start, but are ignored. Kate, for instance, moved in with a man from a different culture, and with a very different attitude towards children. At the time she was desperate for a child, and closed her eyes to the problems which soon made themselves evident. 'We certainly would have parted very early on, if I'd given it more time before becoming pregnant,' she says now. 'But I was impatient for a child by then.' She stayed with her husband for the children's sake, and only left when they reached their teens.

Hilary took her time deciding to marry Philip, her second husband, and then did so against her better judgement. Other stresses and pressures, including her fear of being alone, influenced her. 'I had many misgivings about marrying him. However, my daughter was at A-level stage and I knew she would be going off to college soon and I would have to face living alone, for the first time in my life. My parents lived next door, but my mother died of cancer that same year, after an agonising, drawn-out illness.' Once wed, the problems of her husband's excessive drinking and smoking and his difficult temperament got worse and worse.

Wendy, twice married and living with her third partner, could not have predicted the problems which eventually caused the rift. Her partner changed when he became deeply involved in politics: 'I felt jealous/rejected/hurt/unloved when he began to devote all his time, energy and money to the Party. We discussed the problem at great length (still do). He is stubborn, I get angry.' This came on top of the other great trauma in this relationship: Wendy's jealousy of Rick's daughter by his first marriage. 'He loved his own daughter so much more than mine and showed it. Agony, right from the beginning. I felt jealous, but afraid to admit it.' Perhaps this problem could eventually have been overcome — after all, in time the child would have moved away from home and posed less of a threat. Coupled with Rick's all-absorbing entanglement in politics, however, it tipped the balance of Wendy's tolerance level beyond the limit and the relationship collapsed.

Russell cites the only major problem second time around as 'the relationship between my son and my girlfriend. It is she who sees it as a problem rather than me.' However, on investigation it turns out that his girlfriend sees things differently. These are her conclusions, which apparently she has not felt able to share with Russell.

> When I first met Russell he had a lot of serious financial and emotional problems. We fell in love and I saw him through the most difficult time of his life. I fitted the bill perfectly for him — I was unmarried, unattached, independent, sensible, practical and financially stable; the exact opposite of his ex-wife. I was never scared off by the problems surrounding his divorce because I knew that they could be overcome and would not last for ever. When I met his son, however, and began to experience problems with him, I knew that it was different because his son actually would be around for ever.
>
> Russell had also had a vasectomy while he was

married. At first I did not think that having no children would bother me, but since Adam has been coming at weekends I have become resentful that I have to make allowances in my life for a child who is not mine and who gives me nothing in return.

The problems with Adam have thrown the whole future of our relationship into question as far as I am concerned, although I know that Russell does not feel the same way. He would like us to get married but I cannot commit myself to him, knowing that this also means saddling myself with Adam. We are still together because I suppose I am unwilling to admit failure and probably still cherish a hope that things will improve.

A huge gulf exists here which can only begin to be bridged if Russell admits that there is a problem. So far he has seemed unwilling or unable to do this and the future for the two of them looks bleak.

Diana admits that she married for the first time to get away from her parents. The marriage was never a success and the problems escalated when her husband met someone else. Both came away from the experience very embittered, and Diana felt depressed and very lonely. She hated living alone, and married the first man she met after separating. Problems arose immediately which must have been apparent before the marriage took place. Reading between the lines Diana seems a deeply unhappy and bitter woman in a relationship where failure is almost inevitable. She has nothing good to say about her second husband nor, for that matter about herself.

I have been depressed and seeing a family therapist because of problems with my stepsons. My husband is not supportive in regard to this. He is cold and uncommunicative, just like my first husband. I have learned nothing from the experience of my divorce and feel sure I have made another mistake . . . I feel as if I have never been able to like myself or my own company.

The wounds from Diana's separation had hardly begun to heal when she met her second husband. She fell headlong into the trap of remarrying to escape the misery of a lonely single life. If she could learn to like herself more, and work out *why* she keeps repeating her mistakes, she might stand a better chance of making a happier relationship in future.

Jenny felt resentful right through her first marriage. She had married because she was pregnant and the marriage was a failure from the word go. Both she and her husband were unfaithful and after the split she married the man with whom she was having an affair. There are two children of the second marriage. Although the couple are still together, Jenny is not happy.

> I married because of fear. Often a bad second marriage is less frightening to a woman than no marriage at all. I have learned a great deal about sharing, controlling my temper and managing financially in this marriage, but although I am a much steadier person I am still very resentful underneath. I would like to bring up my children on my own now. I feel more mature, thank God, and can support them financially. But they are very fond of their father and I feel it would be unfair to separate them at this time (or am I still afraid?).

LOOKING BACK, LOOKING FORWARD

It's wellnigh impossible to cast off the past without a backward glance. Many second-timers express regrets about their first marriages but, rather than wishing they had stayed put, many wish they had left earlier, or had not married their ex in the first place. Others regret that things ended badly, or are sorry about the pain that was caused to everyone involved. And some regret that the marriage had ended at all — not, however, necessarily wishing they were still in it. For those now in a happy relationship, or struggling to keep together a less than satisfactory marriage, there is an obvious commitment to the future as a couple.

But how do those who are on their own again feel about the whole institution of marriage? Are they bitter, or would they try it again if the chance arose? Kate now lives alone after her second divorce, although until recently her two teenage children lived with her.

I think I'm far better off on my own. I can't bear men round me all the time. There is a time when you're young when it all seems right, but having gone through that and it didn't work I certainly don't think I could go through it again. After that first let down, when I discovered that my first husband had lied to me about his debts, I never felt the same about marriage again. And anyway I'm not sure what there is to be gained from it. It is lovely to have a man in your bed, but not every night. Mind you, when I'm about 70 . . . one doesn't want to end up alone, drawn and wrinkled; solitary and miserable. But equally one doesn't want to end up with an irritating man snoring and coughing and having to be nursed. It sounds awfully selfish, but I feel strongly about that.

I know I'm very difficult, and I don't think the man exists that I could permanently settle down with. If he does, the odds are I'll never meet him. It doesn't bother me, feeling like that. It would if I didn't know any men, and have men that I'm attached to — that level of involvement suits me fine. My philosophy is that a 24-hour day is as much as I can cope with and I don't look to the future.

There is one other factor. I felt I couldn't have another relationship with a man while the kids were still at home. I couldn't inflict another man on my children. From what I've seen of step-families, they don't work. It would be just another whole set of problems.

Hilary is now 60 and has been alone for three and a half years.

There has until recently been very little communication

between Philip and me. The intervening years have at times meant much loneliness for each of us, and we have now started to write to each other. So, in spite of a legal separation that has just taken effect, it may not be the end of the story. I would say, however, that it is almost impossible to escape the problems of the first marriage affecting the second one. If there are children from previous marriages it is even harder.

Like Hilary, Wendy is still in touch with her estranged partner. Their separation is far more recent, and the relationship is still going through its death throes, although it seems unlikely that the two will be able to get back together. Wendy feels that she has learned much from her relationships, and retains a sense of optimism for the future, in spite of the pain of the present separation.

The first time I married I was ridiculously young and naive. Then I put my second husband on a pedestal from which he soon crashed down. I know now that kindness and tolerance are more important in a partner than dynamism. I became very independent, self-sufficient, tough. I now realise that what I feel for somebody is more important than worrying about what they feel for me.

The set-up now changes all the time because I'm never really content. When Rick first went I got a new boyfriend straight away and saw him every day and that lasted a few months. And when he went off the scene I fell back into Rick's arms. He's always there if I want him. He welcomes me with open arms; he's always very sweet. But we went out on Friday and I stayed the night and expected we'd spend Saturday together, but he said, 'I'm busy now with political work.' I was ever so upset. I shouted at him as I left the house, 'I feel just the same as I did that night before you left.' It's all still there, the caring for him and the resentment all combined. We've slept together three times in the last fortnight and I'm more muddled than ever. I keep thinking that as time passes I'll feel better. But it's not different at all. There are physical things you like about someone and that doesn't change.

Yes, I would marry again. Every time I've gone into a new situation it's always been worthwhile; an awful lot's come out of it. I don't think I regret any of it. I regret my own childlike emotions, that's all. And maybe I regret staying with Gerard so long. I didn't develop with him, but I've developed so much with Rick.

WORDS OF WISDOM

To sum up, it's worth quoting, and reiterating, some of the advice from those who've been through it to those who are embarking now on a second relationship:

It is vital to take time to find oneself and recover from wounds of the first relationship before starting on a new relationship — ideally one should wait at least two years. However, if alone for a very long time it can cause difficulties of readjustment the other way. Talk things through carefully and thoroughly with all children concerned, and keep talking.

Move slowly so that you can see if you are repeating the same mistakes.

Don't be in a rush to marry — live together if you must.

Wait. Be brave, spend some time trying to cope alone if you can.

Talk everything over, especially whether or not you want children, before you finally decide.

Talk through the implications of the existence of ex-spouses and children from previous marriages.

If at all possible I would advise people to live together

first before marrying, especially where children are concerned. Children can manipulate and subconsciously destroy a relationship between their parent and new partner.

I would strongly advise anyone getting married to ask themselves why. If it is for financial reasons, or for lifetime 'company' then they are on a sticky road. Marriage requires care, understanding, trust and freedom.

Both partners need their own spaces to be free and develop as well as cuddles and togetherness. Support each other, don't stifle each other and, as much as is possible, don't be affected by outside pressures.

Explore expectations, identify what went wrong in previous relationships.

Insist on getting what's right for you, right from the beginning. If you're not getting that, break up the relationship — that's much better than letting the relationship break you up.

Learn from what went wrong first time.

The one quality I've noticed in long-term happy liaisons is the apparent lack of jealousy.

It's important to be realistic about the past. Just because you got it wrong the first time doesn't mean you won't get it right next time.

Exercise rational caution, but don't give up hope of success despite a first failure. Equally, don't be too starry eyed. *Talk* about issues before they become issues. *Demonstrate* your love for the other person: saying 'I love you', or doing small services, or giving tiny, silly presents spontaneously will help to keep a sense of warmth and vitality, however apparently trivial the occasion.

Be not quite so idealistic; compromise; be not quite so certain that one is always right; be not so sharp-tongued; but also keep a space for oneself that is untouchable and strong, where no one else can penetrate.

Treat the new person as themselves, don't compare them with your previous partner — impossible not to, to some extent, but keep it to a minimum.

Nurture the relationship as you would water a plant, in order to keep it flourishing.

Learning to live together means learning to accept and to trust; it means forgiving yourself and your partner when either of you gets it wrong, and it means trying that bit harder to get it right. See it as a joint, life-long enterprise and an opportunity for permanent enriching change, and you're half-way there.

USEFUL ADDRESSES

Relate (National Marriage Guidance Council)
Herbert Gray College
Little Church Street
Rugby
Warwickshire CV21 3AP
(0788) 73241
Offers help to couples whether or not they are married. Consult your telephone book or the above address for the nearest local office.

Gingerbread (Association for One-Parent Families)
35 Wellington Street
London WC2E 7BN
(01) 240-0953

National Council for One-Parent Families
255 Kentish Town Road
London NW5 2LX
(01) 267-1361

Stepfamily (National Stepfamily Association)
162 Tenison Road
Cambridge
CB1 2DP
(0223) 460312

Westminster Pastoral Foundation
23 Kensington Square
London W8 5HN
(01) 937-6956
Offers counselling individually, in groups, couples or families, for personal, marital or family problems. Will

USEFUL ADDRESSES

give information on affiliated counselling centres in England and Wales.

Institute of Family Therapy
43 New Cavendish Street
London W1M 7RG
(01) 935-1651
Family therapy includes the family as a whole and is offered for a wide range of problems, helping families to share information and find new ways of relating.

Women's Therapy Centre
6 Manor Gardens
London N7 6LA
(01) 263-6200

The British Association for Counselling
37a Sheep Street
Rugby
Warwickshire CV21 3BX
(0788) 78328

The Scottish Association for Counselling
26 Frederick Street
Edinburgh EH2 2JR

Northern Ireland Association for Counselling
93 Laharna Avenue
Larne BT40 1NY

ABOUT THE AUTHOR

Elizabeth Martyn is a full time professional writer. She was formerly on the staff of *Good Housekeeping* magazine, and now writes for various women's magazines.

She married at 20, separated at 29 and divorced two years later. After living alone for three years she met her present partner, and they live together in West London.

All Optima books are available at your bookshop or newsagent, or can be ordered from the following address:

Optima, Cash Sales Department,
PO Box 11, Falmouth, Cornwall TR10 9EN

Please send cheque or postal order (no currency), and allow 60p for postage and packing for the first book, plus 25p for the second book and 15p for each additional book ordered up to a maximum charge of £1.90 in the UK.

Customers in Eire and BFPO please allow 60p for the first book, 25p for the second book plus 15p per copy for the next 7 books, thereafter 9p per book.

Overseas customers please allow £1.25 for postage and packing for the first book and 28p per copy for each additional book.